# 16 Guidelines
### for a
# Happy Life

# 16 Guidelines
## for a
# Happy Life
## the basics

**Alison Murdoch**
**Deyki-Lee Oldershaw**

**Essential Education**

First Published in Great Britain in 2008 by
Essential Education, an initiative of the
Foundation for Developing Compassion and Wisdom
43 Renfrew Road, London SE11 4NA

Illustrations by Robin Stephens, robinstephensart@hotmail.com

ISBN 978-0-9557204-1-3

Typeset by Pantek Arts Ltd, Maidstone, Kent

Printed in the UK

# Contents

# Foreword

Essential Education is an international initiative to help people everywhere develop their natural capacity to be kind and wise. This will be achieved by providing resources, training and support for use in a wide variety of settings: schools, the workplace, prisons, hospices, the home – wherever people live and learn.

## WHY THE 16 GUIDELINES?

In the seventh century CE, the great Tibetan King, Songtsen Gampo had an unexpected change of heart. He abandoned his successful career as a military leader and proceeded to introduce a new legal system, build schools and temples, and invite philosophical and spiritual teachers from neighbouring India to teach people how to be happy.

The *16 Guidelines for a Happy Life* are based on the inspirational values and principles that King Songtsen Gampo introduced to his people. They are 'ideas to make life better', and they played a crucial part in the transformation of Tibet from a warlike nation into a civilisation renowned for its peace and serenity.

We offer this modern re-working of ancient wisdom with the aspiration that it will help to bring about a similar transformation of hearts and minds in the twenty-first century. For more information, please visit *www.16guidelines.org*.

## HOW TO USE THIS BOOK

Like the Guidelines themselves, this book is direct and practical. You can open it at any page. The text is illustrated with quotes, true stories, challenges and reflections to suit different personalities and situations.

The *16 Guidelines for a Happy Life: the basics* is not intended to be comprehensive. Its simple aim is to draw out the wisdom that we all hold inside of ourselves and encourage us to adapt the Guidelines to our own needs and circumstances.

Alison Murdoch, *London*
Dekyi-Lee Oldershaw, *Toronto*

# Acknowledgements

Thanks are due to the following people, whose energy, skills and determination helped to make this publication possible: Michael Adam; Eleanor Brunnen; Federicka Cardelli; Anna Cherry; Martin Cherett; Rasmus Hougaard; Martin Klopstock; Venerable Roger Kunsang; Jane Moore; Venerable Constance Miller; Vicki Mackenzie; Suzy Murdoch; Hannah Pearce and Fiona O'Shaughnessy.

The text design is based on an original design by Richard Blaney.

About the Publication Sponsor: Terrapinn is a business media company whose events, training and publications offer businesses around the world inspiring and rewarding opportunities to experience fresh ideas, network and acquire new skills. Terrapinn employs over 600 people from offices based in London, New York, Singapore, Sydney and Johannesburg.

Special thanks are due to Lama Zopa, who was the original visionary behind the *16 Guidelines for a Happy Life*. He is the Honorary President of the Foundation for Developing Compassion and Wisdom. Essential Education is a Foundation initiative.

# Introduction

Most people spend all their life looking for happiness, in one way or another. Everyone wants to be happy. So why do we give the subject so little direct attention?

In affluent countries, we are surrounded by possessions and material comfort, but where is the real happiness in our lives? We seem to have lost touch with what it means, and how to find it.

The *16 Guidelines for a Happy Life* take a direct and practical approach to the subject of happiness. They propose that everyone has the capacity to be happy. However, this can only be achieved step by step: through sustained effort to relieve the causes of unhappiness, and through paying attention to the well-being of others as well as ourselves. External circumstances can help us in our search for happiness, but they are often a distraction. Happiness is an inner journey.

## COMPASSION AND WISDOM

The *Guidelines* are based on the two underlying principles of compassion and wisdom. Both need to be cultivated: to have one without the other is to fly around in circles like a bird with one wing.

*Compassion* Human beings are sociable creatures, and it is almost impossible to cultivate the qualities described by the *16 Guidelines* in isolation. For example, how can we develop patience without someone or something to annoy us? This also taps into a deeper truth: that the quickest route to happiness may be simply to cherish other people, and to care about their well-being as much, if not more, than our own.

*Wisdom* Lasting happiness is dependent on a realistic approach to how we function as human beings, and a robust understanding of the world around us. On this basis, the *16 Guidelines* propose that we pay particular attention to four strategies:

- How we think – the power of the mind
- How we act – every action brings a result
- How we relate to others – we are all deeply interconnected
- How we find meaning – if everything is changing, anything is possible

The *16 Guidelines for a Happy Life* are:

- *Universal* They address the nature and potential of human beings, beyond any differences of race, creed or culture. This is why they repeatedly appear in the spiritual, religious and wisdom traditions of the world.

- *Powerful* The minute we follow the *Guidelines*, our lives change. But they demand sincerity and perseverance. We need to explore their meaning and put them into practice because they make sense to us, not because someone else tells us to do so.

- *Infinitely adaptable* The *Guidelines* can be our companion through all stages and circumstances of our lives, and there is always more to explore. They are relevant to every situation, particularly when we want to help others and bring about change.

## THE 16 ROLE MODELS

The role models in this book provide contemporary examples of how each Guideline can manifest in a person's behaviour and life choices and unleash immense potential.

In researching their lives and achievements, it quickly became apparent that each role model exemplifies most, if not all, of the *Guidelines*. The *Guidelines* overlap and are interconnected – each one leads to all the others.

Each of the 16 role models has found a profound degree of happiness and serenity for themselves despite – or because of – their willingness to engage with the most pressing issues of their time. This offers reassurance that through practising the *16 Guidelines* we can each, in our own way, help to bring peace and happiness into the world.

# HOW WE THINK

# Change your mind, change your life

How we think lies at the root of every word we speak and every action we perform – where we live, who we choose as our friends, what job we do and how we spend our time. Our lives are shaped by our thoughts from earliest childhood until the day we die. For this reason, recognising the power of the mind is the most important theme that underlies the *16 Guidelines for a Happy Life.*

It is a natural instinct to experience the world as something 'out there'. This focus on external circumstances makes us vulnerable to their ebb and flow, which can never be completely in our favour. However, if you probe more deeply, it becomes clear that your experience of the world is significantly affected by what is going on 'inside' – by your state of mind.

One day, to see a man and woman embracing in public can make you feel relaxed and happy. On another, you might feel envious and miserable. We are also influenced by our cultural conditioning. In one country, an embrace between a man and a woman, whether married or not, is regarded as a natural show of affection. In another, it may be considered immoral and unacceptable. Our emotional reactions are driven by a complex mixture of experiences, attitudes and beliefs.

If you pause to consider, you can recognise that behind every emotion lies a thought. We are often not conscious of this, because events happen so quickly. An outburst of anger might come from the thought 'this person frightens me', 'I'm going to get hurt' or 'I can't get what I want'. When we are depressed, thoughts can pile up relentlessly: 'I'm not good enough', 'I've made such a mess of things', 'no one likes me' or 'this will never come to an end'. Even if the thoughts are exaggerated or untrue, our minds have the power to create a downward spiral of misery and dissatisfaction.

Therein, however, also lies an opportunity. Just as an athlete trains her body, we can train and transform our minds, and in doing so shift our habitual patterns and explore new ways of living. Cultivating humility, patience, contentment and delight offers us four ways to achieve this.

'I LONG TO ACCOMPLISH GREAT AND NOBLE TASKS, BUT IT IS MY CHIEF DUTY TO
ACCOMPLISH HUMBLE TASKS AS THOUGH THEY WERE GREAT AND NOBLE'
HELEN KELLER, USA

# 01 HUMILITY

## WHAT IS HUMILITY?

Humility is the attitude of experiencing the world and what it contains with wonder and awe. It is about seeing ourselves as a small part of a vast cosmos, inhabited by people and creatures from whom we can learn.

Humility is quiet strength. In some cultures it is considered quite normal to be loud and assertive about what we think and what we want. Yet there is something dignified about people who are sincerely humble. Even if they are prominent and successful, they have the wisdom and experience to understand their limitations.

A person with humility can see beyond their own viewpoint and interests. They acknowledge that we are all dependent on other people, and that we have unique and sometimes unexpected roles to play in each other's lives. Humility shifts our perspective from 'me' to 'others' and is delighted to do so.

Humility comes at the beginning of the *16 Guidelines* because it is a starting point. How can we grow and develop if we think we have nothing to learn?

## WHY HELEN KELLER?

Helen Keller achieved worldwide recognition as a speaker and campaigner while remaining in touch with her isolation, vulnerability and dependence on others. Growing up in Alabama, USA, she lost her hearing and sight at the age of 18 months. Despite the challenges she faced, she worked tirelessly not only to promote the rights of disabled people but also in support of issues such as poverty, racism, birth control and women's rights.

'No-one knows better than I the bitter denials of life. But I have made my limitations tools of learning and true joy,' Helen Keller said at the age of 80. Having worked through so many obstacles herself, she was determined to help other people do the same. 'I do not like the world as it is; so I am trying to make it a little more as I want it.'

Helen Keller's energy was extraordinary. She spoke on the subject of disability in over 35 different countries, and began a 40,000-mile tour of Asia when she was

75 years old. She met with 10 United States presidents, was the first deaf-blind individual to receive a Bachelor of Arts degree in the USA, and the first woman to receive an honorary degree from Harvard University. She was the subject of an Academy-Award winning documentary and of a Broadway play. More than 1200 mourners attended her funeral. Yet she had enough detachment from her own achievements to describe her hospital visits to the blind, deaf and disabled soldiers of World War II as 'the crowning experience of my life.'

**'TO SAY YOU DON'T KNOW IS THE BEGINNING OF KNOWING'**
**CHINESE PROVERB**

Ironically, Helen Keller herself remarked, 'I believe humility is a virtue, but I prefer not to use it unless it is absolutely necessary.' Is the person who shuns humility the one who best embodies it? It seems logical that those who consider themselves humble are in more danger of being proud and pleased with themselves. As Benjamin Franklin observed, 'Alas, I know if I ever became truly humble, I would be proud of it'.

## HOW DOES HUMILITY LEAD TO HAPPINESS?

Humility arises when our defences are stripped away – those thoughts that whisper to tell us that we are unique or special; that we are under threat or being judged; that we need to protect ourselves. Humility allows us to admit that we are fearful and vulnerable, that we don't always get it right, and don't always know what to do. This can often create the conditions for self-acceptance and for inner calm.

A person with humility has the intelligence to recognise: that we are all completely dependent on each other; that what we consume depends on a web of connections across the globe; that we all depend on practical and emotional support from others for our existence. To realise this is to be in touch with reality.

**'I NEVER MET A MAN SO IGNORANT THAT I COULDN'T LEARN SOMETHING FROM HIM'** GALILEO GALILEI, ITALY

Extraordinary things can follow from this more gentle confidence. When we enter a room that is full of people - like a meeting or a party - there is a choice. We can walk in full of brittle anxiety about how to behave and how we want people to relate to us. 'Here I am!' Or we can try 'There you are!' Being soft and flexible, needing nothing from anyone, taking a genuine interest in the unique character and viewpoints of those around us.

When we are scared or anxious, there is a natural urge to tighten up and take refuge in pride or self-importance. Is it possible to alter this behaviour? Can we instead learn to open up and become more sensitive and flexible? If we behave in a

**TRUE STORY:** In 1978 the Russian virtuoso pianist Vladimir Horowitz was invited to play Rachmaninov's third piano concerto to a select audience at Carnegie Hall, New York City. The concerto was one of his favourite pieces of music – he had been playing it for nearly thirty years – and the performance was phenomenal. The virtuosity and technical skill of the master pianist left the audience spellbound. After the performance, a young piano student nervously came up to ask a question. 'Sir, how long have you taken to prepare this piece?' Horowitz replied 'I am still working on it!'

humble and relaxed manner, it encourages other people to respond in the same way. It has the unexpected power to transform even the most difficult of situations.

Great masters of the martial art Aikido teach humility through skilful moves which aim to disarm the opponent so that neither person is harmed. One particular movement is described as 'walking in another's shoes'. When a person makes a challenge, their wrist is grasped, and then both people turn and move in the same direction. The momentum of this forceful action moves both people forward. In doing this an opponent's

'HUMILITY IS NOT A PECULIAR HABIT OF SELF-EFFACEMENT, RATHER LIKE HAVING AN INAUDIBLE VOICE. IT IS A SELFLESS RESPECT FOR REALITY' IRIS MURDOCH, UK

negative energy is transformed into something positive. Apply this to life and we can find ourselves walking beside our surprised opponent, in their position, experiencing their viewpoint.

In most areas of work and in our private lives, success collects around the people who have the confidence to listen to views that contrast with their own. Increasingly, it is important to seek information and advice from other people in the areas where we lack expertise. The humble person will put aside the idea that they are being threatened or belittled. Whereas someone who is proud and disdainful may fail to get the feedback they need.

One consequence of thinking that we are superior to the people around us is that we lose the ability to listen. What a terrible loss, when we have so much to learn from each other. There is a Tibetan saying which compares the person with pride to an upturned pot: it cannot let anything in and it cannot be filled.

If we continue to add layers of pride, like layers of varnish, we become more hardened. It can be very difficult to return to a state of humility. Sometimes it takes a personal tragedy, such as illness or bereavement, to crack open the shell we have built up.

When encountering someone who is puffed up with pride, no matter how beautiful they look or how well they speak, instinct can make us draw back. We often attempt to bring them back down to earth. The media can be at its most cruel towards the people who are seen to be full of pride.

**'THE ONLY TRUE WISDOM IS IN KNOWING THAT YOU KNOW NOTHING' SOCRATES, GREECE**

When we read about or encounter someone who has humility, we will often be attracted to them. We want to listen to what they say and to be with them. It creates closeness. They inspire us to believe that we can each make a worthwhile contribution of our own.

Many of the role models in this book have illuminated the quality of humility. It did not get in the way of what they achieved. Rather, it was a source of strength that brought them more respect and a greater power to influence others.

**CHALLENGE:** When people try to speak with you, do you sometimes continue with what you are doing, such as cooking a meal, reading a newspaper or looking at a computer screen? Do you treat them as if they were not important enough to have your full attention? Next time this happens, stop what you are doing. Make eye contact and listen carefully. Note one new thing that you have learned.

## REFLECTION

- Find a quiet space where you can relax. Sit comfortably. To help you settle, focus your awareness on your breathing. Let go of any thoughts, images or feelings that arise. Whenever you become distracted, bring your awareness gently back to the sensation of the breath going in and out. Spend a few minutes enjoying the experience of coming to rest.

- Observe your mind in an objective way, as if you were watching a movie. Keep a sense of distance between you as the viewer, and the movie screen. Allow your thoughts to come and go of their own accord as you watch them on the screen. Take your time and wait for the activity to slow down. Resist engaging with your thoughts.

- You may notice strong emotions such as resentment, jealousy or romantic love flooding the screen. They may even suck you in, until you are no longer the viewer but an actor in the movie. If this happens, extract yourself slowly and gently, and return to watching it from afar.

- How does the flavour and intensity of your emotions change on the screen? Observe them carefully, while still taking care not to identify with them. Do they make you feel bigger and stronger, or more fearful and vulnerable? How do they affect your self image? Give yourself time to observe your responses as if you were watching a movie.

- Until now you have been the viewer. Next switch to being the commentator. What does this process tell you about who you are? Explore questions such as: How realistic is my self image? Is it accurate and helpful, or is it simply a projection of the mind? What is there to be proud or arrogant about? Can I be more relaxed about who I am?

- What can you learn from this experience? Whatever conclusion you arrive at, sit with it for a while and just let it deepen.

- Close with the wish 'May all beings be happy!'

## RESOURCES

The Helen Keller Archives are managed by The American Foundation for the Blind. www.afb.org.

Helen Keller wrote twelve books including an early autobiography The Story of My Life (1903; many subsequent editions) and Light in My Darkness with Ray Silverman (new edition, Westchester, PA: Swedenborg Foundation, 2006).

The original text of The Story of My Life is currently free on-line to commemorate the 100th anniversary of its original publishing at www.afb.org/mylife.

'The Miracle Worker', starring Anne Bancroft, directed by Arthur Penn, won two Oscars in 1962 (released on DVD by MGM Studios, 2004).

'Shining Soul: Helen Keller's Spiritual Life and Legacy', directed by Penny Price (released on DVD by the Swedenborg Foundation, 2006).

'MANY PEOPLE THINK THAT TO BE PATIENT IS A SIGN OF WEAKNESS. I THINK THAT IS A
MISTAKE. IT IS ANGER THAT IS A SIGN OF WEAKNESS'
HH THE DALAI LAMA, TIBET

# 02 PATIENCE

## WHAT IS PATIENCE?

To practise patience is to taste the power of the mind. Life is full of uncomfortable experiences, from minor niggles and irritations to major confrontations and setbacks. When they happen, we have a choice about how to respond. We can either become agitated and upset, or we can stay calm and relaxed. Patience is the ability to control our reactions and retain our peace of mind.

Patience gives us the flexibility and strength not to be a victim of circumstance. It is like having a protective suit of armour. It doesn't make us passive or resigned, or take away the ability to respond appropriately to difficulties and harm. On the contrary, patience makes it far more likely we can respond in an appropriate way, because we retain the ability to think clearly.

Some people seem to be born patient, just as others seem to have a tendency to get angry. However, it is also possible to cultivate patience. We can remind ourselves of the damage that is caused by uncontrolled anger. We can accept that an injury may not have been intended. We can remember that the situation will change. Patience is a learning curve that lays the foundations for a happy life.

## WHY THE DALAI LAMA?

The 14th Dalai Lama, Tenzin Gyatso, was awarded the Nobel Peace Prize thirty years after he fled into exile from his native Tibet. Despite the complete takeover of his country by China, huge loss of life, the destruction of thousands of monasteries and the relentless damage caused to wildlife and the environment over many decades, he has consistently sought a peaceful and mutually beneficial resolution with the Chinese government.

The Dalai Lama has often said that the Chinese are his greatest friends, because they have given him the gift of patience. 'Those who would harm us are in a sense teachers of patience. Such people teach us what we could never learn merely from hearing someone speak, be they ever so wise or holy.'

Despite suffering personal hardship, and listening on a daily basis to the heart-rending stories from the Tibetan refugees who arrive to see him, the Dalai Lama remains at peace with himself and the world. His primary response remains one of love rather than anger.

On 1 January 2000, the Dalai Lama presented a special millennial appeal for 'internal disarmament' as the precondition for world peace. He defined internal disarmament as ridding ourselves of all the negative emotions that result in violence. 'There is no need for temple or church, for mosque or synagogue, no need for complicated philosophy, doctrine or dogma. Our own heart, our own mind is the temple.'

Some of the exiled Tibetan community feel that the Dalai Lama has taken the practice of patience to an unhelpful extreme. They would prefer to retaliate against the Chinese occupation of their country with anger and violence. It is impossible to know whether that strategy would be effective in shifting the political stalemate between the two governments. However, the Dalai Lama argues that even if violence seems to have a positive effect in the short term, it leaves a long term legacy of bitterness and hatred that is hard to undo.

## HOW DOES PATIENCE LEAD TO HAPPINESS?

The benefits of patience are extraordinary. On a personal level, it helps us to feel safe, valued and supported. We can share our thoughts and enjoy each other's company without fear of being abused or attacked. It lays an essential foundation for the happiness of individuals and society.

**'YOU CAN'T SHAKE HANDS WITH A CLENCHED FIST'**
**INDIRA GANDHI, INDIA**

Patience starts with each one of us. Imagine never getting irritated or angry again. Of not feeling your buttons pushed and your mind going dark and closed. Never again feeling your body tense up, your fists clench and your face contort. Or not obsessing in the middle of the night about what someone did or didn't say.

Being calm and patient is more efficient than getting angry, even when someone intentionally hurts us. Patience doesn't mean we cannot take counter measures, for their safety and protection as well as for ours. But anything we can manage to do in a calm and patient manner is likely to be more effective than words or actions that come from an angry and uncontrolled mind.

Once anger has got going, it is hard to control what happens next or who gets hurt. It can leave a trail of regret and damaged relationships from generation to generation. At its worst it can lead to violence and war. It takes a very deep patience to move on from what has happened and break the cycle.

**TRUE STORY:** In April 1999, three-year-old Isabel Maude suffered multiple organ failure and cardiac arrest as a result of doctors failing to recognise the life-threatening symptoms of Necrotising Fasciitis, a bacterium that rapidly eats the flesh. Isabel survived, but was left with a large wound around the stomach and groin area requiring extensive plastic surgery. Her parents, Charlotte and Jason Maude, decided not to sue the National Health Service over her treatment. 'We live in a blame culture where people now assume that if anything goes wrong you should sue. Yes, Isabel would have a rough time because of her surgery and subsequent deformity, but money wasn't going to help. By suing we would only have succeeded in putting doctors off medicine. It seemed somehow vindictive. We have forgiven the doctors for not spotting the potentially fatal symptoms. These newly qualified young doctors just don't have the experience to diagnose fatally sick children.' Instead, working with the paediatric consultant who helped save Isabel's life, they have set up Isabel Healthcare (www.isabelhealthcare.com) to help medical professionals around the world to reduce errors in diagnosis and improve patient care.

Reproduced with permission from The Forgiveness Project. **www.theforgivenessproject.com**

Patience depends on us accepting what 'is', here and now, instead of getting angry and upset. It's not easy. We do not seem designed for contentment, either mentally or physically. Our bodies come up with urges and quirks every five minutes, and our minds are quick to take offence. Patience demands the flexibility and wisdom to accept that we can't always have things our way, and that change may take time.

'DO YOU HAVE PATIENCE TO WAIT TILL YOUR MUD SETTLES AND THE WATER IS CLEAR? CAN YOU REMAIN UNMOVING TILL THE RIGHT ACTION ARISES BY ITSELF?'

LAO TZU, CHINA

Often we learn the most from uncomfortable situations, providing we are willing to stay the course. It takes a special kind of patience to allow events to come to maturity and to be fulfilled. To be open to the unexpected outcome, rather than the one we might originally have pushed for.

'If a situation upsets you and you can change it, then do so! If you can't change it, then stop worrying about it!' advises the Dalai Lama. Yet, how often do we get angry about something that is inevitable, such as illness or even death?

It is a characteristic of anger to seem wholly justifiable. Yet the range of things that make us upset suggests that anger has its roots more in our thoughts than in anything 'out there.' The incident that disturbs our peace of mind on Monday may not bother us on Tuesday, or next month. For one person it is infuriating, for another it is no big deal. All it takes is a shift of perspective for the whole picture to change.

The real work of patience happens in the quiet moments: when we have removed ourselves from the person or the situation that upsets us; when it's possible to take a deep breath and let go of tangled feelings; when we can find the space and honesty to admit that we may have acted unskilfully ourselves.

An eighth century Indian teacher called Shantideva commented that since there will always be things that irritate and annoy us, it's better to cover our own feet with leather rather than attempt to make the whole world smooth and comfortable for ourselves.

**'I WOULD NOT LOOK UPON ANGER AS SOMETHING FOREIGN TO ME THAT I HAVE TO FIGHT...I HAVE TO DEAL WITH MY ANGER WITH CARE, WITH LOVE, WITH TENDERNESS, WITH NON-VIOLENCE'**
**THICH NHAT HANH, VIETNAM**

Is it possible to change our habits? If we have enough determination, every provocation can become a challenge – not to give in to our annoyance, but to conquer it. It is impossible to learn patience unless there is something that irritates us. To expect life to go smoothly is to miss the point.

**CHALLENGE:** Is there anyone who really irritates you? Take five minutes out, in a quiet spot, to identify exactly what gets on your nerves. Is there a quality in that person which you have a hard time accepting within yourself? Can you use this insight to bring some space into the situation?

## REFLECTION

- Find a quiet space where you can relax. Sit comfortably. To help you settle, focus your awareness on your breathing. Let go of any thoughts, images or feelings that arise. Whenever you become distracted, bring your awareness gently back to the sensation of the breath going in and out. Spend a few minutes enjoying the experience of coming to rest.

- Allow yourself to connect with the patience and compassion that exist deep within your heart. Imagine your heart overflowing with these qualities and taste the peace that they bring.

- Identify someone with whom you are having difficulty at the moment. Imagine that they are standing in front of you and gently accept their presence. If this is hard to do, go back to watching your breath for a few minutes until you feel relaxed again. Be gentle with yourself and with them. Can you maintain a sense of patience and compassion in your heart?

- Now remember a time when they spoke or behaved in a way that you found challenging or disturbing. Imagine the agitated emotions that were running through their mind. Allow yourself to explore the suffering that *they* were going through. Proceed slowly and gently, in a spirit of patience and compassion.

- Recall a time when you felt anger, jealousy or any other disturbing emotion towards this person. How did that feel in your heart? What effect did it have on you? What impact did it have on them? Did either of you gain from that situation?

- Now imagine that the person is trying to have an argument with you. As an experiment, decide that you are willing to lose the argument, that you won't answer back, score points, or attempt to control how they behave. Do your best to be genuinely kind, open, patient and compassionate.

- Trust in and enjoy the process. How did it feel?

- Close with the wish 'May all beings be happy!'

## RESOURCES

www.dalailama.com is the official website of The Dalai Lama, who is based in Dharamsala, India.

The 14th Dalai Lama, Ancient Wisdom, Modern World: Ethics for the New Millennium (London: Little, Brown, 1999) outlines his secular vision.

The 14th Dalai Lama, Freedom in Exile: Autobiography of His Holiness the Dalai Lama (London: Abacus, 1998).

The 14th Dalai Lama, Healing Anger: The Power of Patience from a Buddhist Perspective (Ithaca, N.Y.: Snow Lion Publications, 1997).

'Kundun' starring Tenzin Thuthob Sarong, directed by Martin Scorsese, 1998 (released on DVD by Buena Vista Home Entertainment, 2004).

'THERE IS ENOUGH IN THE WORLD FOR EVERYONE'S NEED, BUT NOT FOR ANYONE'S GREED'
MAHATMA GANDHI, INDIA

# 03 CONTENTMENT

When all the trees have been cut down,
when all the animals have been hunted,
when all the waters are polluted,
when all the air is unsafe to breathe,
only then will you discover you cannot eat money.
Cree Prophecy, North America

## WHAT IS CONTENTMENT?

Contentment is a state of mind that has nothing to do with money, objects, or other
people. Nor does it concern itself with how much we have, or how little. Instead,
it's about finding a point of stillness within ourselves which allows us to be quietly
happy whatever our situation might be, and to be at peace with who we are.

How do you experience contentment? It can be as easy – and yet as radical – as
taking a breath in, and deciding to release everything that makes us feel anxious and
dissatisfied as you breathe out. Try settling deeply and quietly in a traffic jam, in the
middle of an argument, or when tears are close. Let the commotion of the world
simply come to rest. Is it possible to taste the experience of surrender and release?

Unless we learn to live in the moment, and to accept it as it is, we may never
function well or feel fully alive. Contentment releases us from the restless desires
that drive us blindly forward, and which prevent us from being open to the needs
and gifts of others. It frees us up to direct our energy in fresh and more conscious
ways. Can we discover how to enjoy contentment despite the hurry and worry of
our contemporary existence?

## WHY MAHATMA GANDHI?

Mahatma Gandhi gave up his career as a lawyer to campaign for justice and peace
in areas such as the alleviation of poverty, religious tolerance, economic self-
sufficiency, the rights of the 'untouchables' and - above all – for 'swaraj', Indian
independence from foreign domination. However, his greatest legacy lies not
solely in his actions but in the way he chose to live. This is why he became known
as the 'Mahatma' or 'great soul'.

Gandhi was intensely interested in the issue of contentment, which he associated with a return to traditional values and a simpler way of life. 'There is more to life than increasing its speed', he said. He combined the role of an international statesman with a highly disciplined spiritual life that included lifelong vegetarianism, spending one day each week in

**'CONTENTMENT IS NATURAL WEALTH; LUXURY IS ARTIFICIAL POVERTY' SOCRATES, GREECE**

silence, living as a celibate, and undergoing frequent fasts. 'My life is my message', he said. 'We must be the change we want to see in the world.'

The most visible and memorable example of Gandhi's personal commitment to simplicity was his decision to adopt the traditional Indian loincloth or *dhoti* as his style of dress. He also chose to weave it himself. On a visit to the UK, he was accused of being disrespectful for not wearing more clothes at a meeting with King Edward VIII. 'The King was wearing enough for both of us!' was his response.

Gandhi's commitment to simplicity permeated his life. In the political arena, it was a symbol of the differences between traditional Indian values and those of the British colonisers. In the social and economic sphere, he encouraged Indians to respect each other as equals, irrespective of caste, wealth or religious observance. He was also a passionate advocate of environmental sustainability.

Simplicity is not the same as contentment, although the two qualities often reinforce each other. It can be argued that Gandhi was never content with the political or economic developments that India went through in his lifetime. He could be judgemental about himself and about other people, and was always ready to speak up and campaign for change. However he combined this with a deep level of personal contentment which seems to have underpinned his capacity to be active in the world.

## HOW DOES CONTENTMENT LEAD TO HAPPINESS?

Is there anyone who does not yearn to be content? The simple expressions 'I am doing my best' or 'It's ok, you've done all that you could' are some of the kindest words we can ever say to ourselves or to our friends and colleagues.

Contentment brings a quiet joy that spreads into a gentle smile and softened eyes. It comes from a still inner place where everything seems to belong and there is no urge to speak or reach out, unless there is good reason to do so. Someone who is deeply contented has no need to hurt another or to profit at their expense. Family and friends who recognise this peacefulness and harmlessness are drawn to it for rest and refuge. It is often irresistible.

**TRUE STORY:** A shy 36 year-old Aboriginal tribal leader called Jeffrey Lee has turned his back on the opportunity to be one of the richest men in the world. An international nuclear power company wants to extract 14,000 tons of uranium in an area called Koongarra, of which he is the custodian. The uranium would be worth more than five billion Australian dollars. 'I'm not interested in money. I've got a job. I can buy tucker. I can go fishing and hunting. That's all that matters to me' says Lee. He is trying to ensure that this ecologically sensitive land will never be mined. 'This is my country, look, it's beautiful and I fear somebody will disturb it.'

Lindsay Murdoch for **The Age**, Melbourne © 2007, **The Age** Newspaper, Melbourne.

Contentment is not something intellectual, in our head. It is a settled feeling that rests deep inside. It only exists in the single moment of time when we decide to be content with who we are, what we're doing and what we have. Even if the mind continues to buzz gently around at a superficial level, it may be possible for another deeper part of us to be happy and at peace.

Contentment is the cooling influence that enables you to focus our energy and to quiet the feeling of 'not good enough' that can sabotage success. In contrast, discontent is like a parrot on our

**'ASPIRE NOT TO HAVE MORE, BUT TO BE MORE' ARCHBISHOP OSCAR ROMERO, EL SALVADOR**

shoulder that distracts us with its endless inner monologue. How are you feeling? Arc you too hot or too cold? Do you want to get out of bed, or would you rather stay where you are? What do you want to eat for breakfast? Exhausting. Distracting. Unending.

Lack of contentment has chilling consequences. Our habits as discontented consumers have placed the very survival of the planet at risk. Our difficulty in sustaining relationships has led to loneliness and family breakdown. Our inability as nations to co-exist peacefully has created a culture of militarism that even reaches into space.

The habit of wanting more can endlessly clutter and distract our minds. Desire works with a multiplier effect - ever more, even faster – until we are unaware of anything except the object or sensation of being pursued. In our dissatisfied minds, the party that we missed or the relationship that didn't work out becomes the best, the most exciting and the most glittering.

'Less desire means less pain' says Lama Zopa Rinpoche, a Tibetan Buddhist teacher. When we notice that we are exaggerating and obsessing, this is a signal to stop and pause. What is really going on? Our inner wisdom tells us that this kind of relentless wishing and hoping will never bring us peace.

An obsession with everyday details often masks an undercurrent of discontent and a sadness deep inside that can feel like it has been there forever. Constantly grumbling about our commute to work, our love life or our family usually means we are actually unhappy with ourselves. There is a tendency to expend our energy on feeding that discomfort instead of seeking resolution.

Throughout history, spiritual teachers have advocated periods of reduced consumption and voluntary simplicity. In modern life, it can start with turning off a mobile phone or choosing to do less at the weekend. For others, a routine that creates quiet personal time at the beginning or end of the day can have the same effect.

Some people will choose to go 'on retreat' to find a temporary break from the food, drink, conversations, books, TV and shopping that call out to us. Peaceful places can help our thoughts slow down to the point where, momentarily at least, we feel no need to reach for something more.

**'ANY INTELLIGENT FOOL CAN MAKE THINGS BIGGER, MORE COMPLEX AND MORE VIOLENT. IT TAKES A TOUCH OF GENIUS – AND A LOT OF COURAGE – TO MOVE IN THE OPPOSITE DIRECTION'**
E. F. SCHUMACHER, GERMANY

Contentment is easily misunderstood. It isn't about being static, in a world where everything is constantly in flux. Nor is it about being inactive: it can actually free us up to focus more sharply on what is working well. It does not make us weak or passive: on the contrary, as the mind becomes more pliable and open, inspiration and creativity have space to flourish.

A student was once asked by his Tai Chi master to grasp an egg in his hand and, no matter what, not to let it go. She held it tightly in her fist, fingers facing the floor, until her muscles ached. The more the Master reminded the student not to drop the egg, the tighter she held on to it. Finally, the Master took the student's hand and turned it over, gently uncurling her fingers so the egg could rest effortlessly on the opened palm.

**CHALLENGE:** Do you often feel restless and dissatisfied? Next time you experience this, instead of springing into action, come to a standstill. Resist the impulse to eat, drink, smoke, start a conversation or whatever you usually do. Take a few deep breaths and accept things as they are. Let it remain so for five minutes. Does this alter the choices you make?

## REFLECTION

● Find a quiet space where you can relax. Sit comfortably. To help you settle, focus your awareness on your breathing. Let go of any thoughts, images or feelings that arise. Whenever you become distracted, bring your awareness gently back to the sensation of the breath going in and out. Spend a few minutes enjoying the experience of coming to rest.

● Call to mind something to which you are currently attached. This could be food, a person, clothing or a place. See it, hear it, taste it, touch it and feel it. Focus all your attention on the object and observe what happens. Feel the pull that it exerts on your mind. Then, lay it aside.

● Next, call to mind something for which you currently have a strong aversion. This could be some food you find disgusting, a person who irritates you, a place that depresses you, or a song that annoys you. How does the mind react? If it is a taste, imagine rolling it around your tongue; if it is a touch sensation, imagine rubbing it up against your arm. Stay with the feeling of aversion for as long as you can. Observe whatever happens to the mind. Then, lay it aside.

● Try to recall a time when you were perfectly content, like a tree unshaken by the wind. How did this feel? What difference did it make to the way you behaved, and the choices that you made?

● Reflect on the experiences you have just had. How often does your mind get tossed around by the senses? How quickly does it move from one object to another? What effect does this have on your behaviour and your relationships? Would you like to be more peaceful and contented? Sit with whatever conclusions you draw from this exercise and allow them to deepen.

● Close with the wish 'May all beings be happy!'

## RESOURCES

www.mahatma.org.in is the official eArchive and reference library for Mahatma Gandhi.

The Mahatma Gandhi Media and Research Service at www.gandhiserve.org provides extensive writings, audio, video and images, with search facilities.

Gandhi, An Autobiography – The Story of my Experiments with Truth (London: Beacon Press, 2003).

Louis Fischer, The Life of Mahatma Gandhi (London: HarperCollins, 1997).

'Gandhi' starring Ben Kingsley, directed by Richard Attenborough, 1982 (released on DVD by Uca catalogue, 2007).

'EVERY INDIVIDUAL MATTERS. EVERY INDIVIDUAL HAS A ROLE TO PLAY.
EVERY INDIVIDUAL MAKES A DIFFERENCE'
JANE GOODALL, UK

# 04 DELIGHT

## WHAT IS DELIGHT?

Delight is the delicious taste we get when something good happens. Worries fade away, frustration evaporates, and anger disappears when a baby is safely born or a friend passes their exams, when a problem is solved or a conflict resolved. Delight opens the heart.

Delight can change our minds and change our lives. It is a tonic that relieves the pain of envy and shifts the blight of depression. It brings us closer to the people we love and eases the difficulties we have with those people who are further away from us.

It makes such good sense to practise the art of rejoicing that it is strange we often overlook it. Why is bad news sometimes more compelling than good news? Why are we tempted to dwell on what is going wrong rather than what is going right? One drags us down, the other lifts us up.

We have a choice about what to feed our heart and mind. If we can learn to dwell on positive stories and accomplishments we can quickly bring more happiness into the lives of ourselves and others.

## WHY JANE GOODALL?

Jane Goodall has taken delight in the natural world ever since she was born. At the age of eighteen months, her mother Vanne remembered gently dissuading her daughter from taking some worms to bed. A few years later, she frightened the adults by disappearing for hours under some hay in the henhouse to wait for a chicken to lay an egg. 'It was Jane's first animal research programme' her mother commented later.

When the renowned anthropologist and palaeontologist Dr. Louis Leakey met Jane in 1957, he was drawn to her natural capacity for enthusiasm and delight. He had been looking for someone to carry out a study of chimpanzees, and

'I REALLY FEEL SORRY FOR PEOPLE WHO DIVIDE THEIR WHOLE LIFE UP INTO 'THINGS THAT I LIKE' AND 'THINGS THAT I MUST DO.' YOU'RE ONLY HERE FOR A SHORT TIME, MATE. LEARN TO LIKE IT'
RUSSELL CROWE, AUSTRALIA

believed that a mind uncluttered by academia would yield a fresh perspective. It was the breakthrough that Jane had been waiting for. Later on, she would say: 'Chimpanzees have given me so much. The long hours spent with them in the forest have enriched my life beyond measure.'

Dr Goodall has been criticised for giving names rather than numbers to the chimpanzees that she studied at Gombe in Tanzania. However her capacity for joy and empathy has been an essential aspect of her research methodology. The first chimpanzee to lose his fear of Jane during her time at Gombe was the male she had named David Greybeard. She was sitting near him one day when she noticed a palm nut lying on the ground. She held it out for him on the palm of her hand. At first he looked away, but then turned to look into her eyes. He took the nut, dropped it on the ground, and gently squeezed her hand. She has described this simple moment as the most significant experience in her many years of working with chimpanzees.

**'IF YOU WERE ALL ALONE IN THE UNIVERSE WITH NO ONE TO TALK TO, NO ONE WITH WHICH TO SHARE THE BEAUTY OF THE STARS, TO LAUGH WITH, TO TOUCH, WHAT WOULD BE YOUR PURPOSE IN LIFE? IT IS OTHER LIFE, IT IS LOVE, WHICH GIVES YOUR LIFE MEANING'**
MITSUGO SAOTOGE, JAPAN

Believing that 'we have the choice to use our lives to make the world a better place,' Jane gave up her own research to become a social and environmental campaigner. The goal of the Jane Goodall Institute is 'to advance the power of individuals to take informed and compassionate action to improve the environment of all living things'. She has also set up an international youth initiative called Roots and Shoots. She says 'my greatest source of hope for the future is the energy, commitment and often the courage of young people when they know the problems and are empowered to act. They are changing the world'.

## HOW DOES DELIGHT LEAD TO HAPPINESS?

Every day, countless opportunities arise to enjoy the positive things that are happening around us. Small children do this naturally – it is often a source of pleasure simply to be with them as they energetically explore and run around. What does it take to re-learn this basic skill?

There is plenty in the world to sadden us, but there is an enormous amount to rejoice about as well. The people who have realised this draw others towards them. Who does not want friends who will be sincerely pleased when good things happen and a tower of positive strength when we get into difficulties? Who will

**TRUE STORY:** In January 2007 a scruffy man in jeans, T-shirt and baseball cap emerged from the subway in Washington DC, USA, and lifted a priceless Stradivarius violin to his chin. It was the height of the morning rush hour, and 1097 people passed by during the 43 minutes that he played six of the most sensational pieces in the violin repertoire. Called Pearls before Breakfast, this was an experiment organised by the Washington Post to see whether Joshua Bell, one of the most accomplished musicians in the world, was capable of distracting people from their headlong rush to work. The answer was pretty much no. It took 6 minutes before anyone stopped, and all he collected was small change. Every time a child walked past they were visibly drawn to the music, but then dragged away by the adult who accompanied them.

Gene Weigarten, 'Pearls Before Breakfast', **The Washington Post**, 8th April 2007 (c) 2007, The Washington Post Writers Group.

not seek the company of those who can cheer us up and take us beyond our habitual worries and concerns? We connect with each other and function best when we can laugh, smile and be open hearted together.

It may be that we grumble and complain the most when life is going well. People seem to learn instinctively how to lift each other's spirits during times of crisis such as war and exile. Those who have survived a tragedy or life threatening illness are often the best at celebration. They pay more attention to the simple pleasures of just 'being alive'.

When we cannot find any joy in everyday pleasures or positive stories, it is a sure sign that we have become trapped in our problems and difficulties. It can be so depressing and exhausting when the mind

**'DREAM AS IF YOU'LL LIVE FOREVER, LIVE AS IF YOU'LL DIE TODAY' JAMES DEAN, USA**

goes round and round obsessively, like an actor learning a negative script or a car stuck on a roundabout. It often takes a fresh perspective to solve the problem. Can we take notice and shift our focus?

Delight not only helps us deal with negative thoughts about ourselves, but also with the painful heavy feelings we can have towards others. Nobody is immune to the stress of competitiveness, or the poison of envy. There is nothing pleasurable in feeling our hands clench, our throat tighten, and our eyes glitter. Bitter comparisons return uninvited to the mind, again and again. Even if they are illogical and unwanted, it is easy to get trapped in a black mood, and lose sight of how to escape.

Delight can move like fresh air through a negative state of mind, bringing spaciousness and ease. Instead of dwelling on what we feel we lack, the challenge is to rejoice quite deliberately in the good fortune of those around us: their health and good looks, their loving family, their beautiful garden or prestigious job. The subject matter is endless – there is always something to delight in. If we can learn to rejoice, our mean-spirited thoughts run out of steam and dissolve away. Each time we taste the thrill of defeating our negative emotions, we will feel better about ourselves. With practice, they may not even arise.

At first, consciously taking delight can sound odd and feel artificial, but the rewards come quickly. At a party or around the coffee station at work, even on a bus or train, we can listen out for what is going well, and relax into enjoying what we hear. If we feel ourselves tighten up when someone talks about getting a promotion or a new car, we can practise being glad for them and dropping the comparisons with ourselves.

Although it manifests as something lighthearted, delight is actually one of the most powerful tools for inner transformation that we possess. When we learn to linger in its warmth, it helps us to gain the confidence and energy to live and behave in the way we most deeply long to do.

**CHALLENGE:** When did you last experience a moment of pure and utter delight? Can you take delight in something that happens today, fully and without reservation? Conclude the day by celebrating these moments instead of dwelling on problems and difficulties.

## REFLECTION

- Find a quiet space where you can relax. Sit comfortably. To help you settle, focus your awareness on your breathing. Let go of any thoughts, images or feelings that arise. Whenever you become distracted, bring your awareness gently back to the sensation of the breath going in and out. Spend a few minutes enjoying the experience of coming to rest.

- Start by rejoicing in all the good things you have done in the past. Think of the positive qualities that you have inside of you - such as kindness, patience and generosity – and the occasions when you have used those qualities to help others. Taste the warmth of appreciation. 'How wonderful it is, how wonderful it is.'

- Gradually broaden your sphere of attention to include the people you feel close to. Rejoice at all their positive qualities and the different ways in which they care for you and for each other. Be as specific as you can. Enjoy the sensation of delight. 'How wonderful it is, how wonderful it is.'

- Move your attention further outwards and rejoice at all the caring actions that are taking place between people you may have never met: teachers in schools, medical staff in hospitals, parents in the home. Is there anyone who does not contribute to the well-being of others in some way?

- Think about the people who campaign for a better world in areas such as justice, equality, peace, poverty or the environment. Recall their contribution. 'How wonderful it is, how wonderful it is.' Reflect on the life stories of the saints of all the different religious traditions, who devoted their lives to spiritual practice and service. Rejoice in their qualities and deeds.

- Finally, see if you can rejoice at all the good things that you and others have done, are doing, and will do in the future. Can you extend this feeling of warmth throughout the whole universe, beyond the bounds of time and space? 'How wonderful it is, how wonderful it is.'

- What would happen if you rejoiced like this on a regular basis?

- Close with the wish 'May all beings be happy!'

## RESOURCES

www.janegoodall.org is the website of the Jane Goodall Institute and www.rootsandshoots.org is the site of its youth programme.

Jane Goodall, In the Shadow of Man (London: Phoenix, 1999) describes the early years of her field research with chimpanzees in Tanzania.

Jane Goodall with Philip Berman, Reason for Hope (Time Warner International, 2005) describes 'the journey of one human being through sixty-five years of earth time'.

Dale Peterson, The Woman Who Redefined Man (Boston: Houghton Mifflin, 2006) is the first official biography of Jane Goodall.

Filmography includes: 'Jane Goodall's Wild Chimpanzees', directed by David Lickley (released on DVD by Sling Shot, 2003) and 'Jane Goodall: Return to Gombe' (released on DVD by Sony Pictures Home Entertainment, 2005).

# HOW WE ACT

# Every skilful action makes a better world

Human lives are composed of nothing but billions of actions - actions of body, speech and mind which take place every minute of the day from the moment of birth until the second when we take our last breath. *How* you choose to act, therefore, defines and colours the very quality of your life and experiences.

Before taking a major decision, such as choosing a job, where to live, or entering a new relationship, most of us will reflect quite carefully on whether it is likely to bring us the happiness we seek. Even when just planning a holiday, we investigate whether it will bring us the comfort, outdoor activities or good company we feel we need. First you think, and then you act. However, we perform countless small actions every day which do not receive this kind of focused attention.

Many small actions are driven by habit. This is most likely why you visit certain shops or restaurants, seek out or avoid different types of people, or read a particular newspaper. From our earliest years, we build up patterns of behaviour, and these bring corresponding results. Just as it takes an apple seed to grow an apple tree, the results of our actions will correspond to the causes that we create. But how often do you review whether your habits and patterns bring the results you seek? Do they still make sense? Will they lead to happiness and satisfaction?

How you choose to act is not only important for your own welfare, but also for that of others. Through our actions we have the choice to nurture friendships, families, community and society – or to bring pain and disharmony. Every little thing we do sets in motion a chain of events. The deeper we probe into this, the stronger is the call to pay intense attention to how we think and subsequently behave, because the consequences can be so complex and far reaching.

Both reason and experience show that certain actions help bring about a greater sense of well-being, while others just create mayhem and misery. Once this is acknowledged, we can no longer simply blame 'the world' or forces outside our control for our circumstances, but must acknowledge our own role in how things are, and take more responsibility for how we behave. Paying attention to the four actions of kindness, honesty, generosity and right speech will lay a solid foundation for contributing to the happiness of ourselves and others.

'THE POVERTY OF THE WEST IS LONELINESS AND INDIFFERENCE. THERE IS HUNGER FOR ORDINARY BREAD, AND THERE IS HUNGER FOR LOVE, FOR KINDNESS AND FOR THOUGHTFULNESS - AND THIS IS THE GREAT POVERTY THAT MAKES PEOPLE SUFFER SO MUCH'

MOTHER TERESA, ALBANIA

# 05 KINDNESS

## WHAT IS KINDNESS?

Kindness says: 'I want you to be happy.' To be kind means to be friendly, caring, generous, benevolent, considerate, respectful, fair and affectionate. We all know in our hearts when we have received or offered kindness because of the warm feeling it brings. Is there anyone who does not want to experience kindness from another person?

Kindness knows with exquisite wisdom when it is appropriate to say or do something. It is found in the small details. A gentle touch on the cheek or a soft support of the elbow guiding someone across the road. Sustaining eye contact for just that moment longer. Making a telephone call. Remembering the little things that please someone.

**'I'VE LEARNED THAT PEOPLE WILL FORGET WHAT YOU SAID, PEOPLE WILL FORGET WHAT YOU DID, BUT PEOPLE WILL NEVER FORGET HOW YOU MADE THEM FEEL'**
**MAYA ANGELOU, USA**

If we act in a kind way, it may seem that we are putting someone else's happiness ahead of ours, but in practice it doesn't work that way. Being kind invariably feels good, lifts our own spirits, and nourishes us in ways that we don't always acknowledge. Everyone benefits.

Is it possible to imagine a world in which everyone shows kindness to each other? Is kindness something we can learn? What can we do to become more kind?

## WHY MOTHER TERESA?

Mother Teresa devoted herself to promoting love and kindness. She founded the Missionaries of Charity specifically to work with people whom everyone else had overlooked. When she was awarded the Nobel Peace Prize, she characteristically diverted the money from the ceremonial banquet to provide a meal for the poor in India. These are just two external manifestations of what became a consuming passion to help others. 'I have found the paradox that if I love until it hurts, then there is no hurt, but only more love' she said.

Although she is now known throughout the world, Mother Teresa's personal acts of kindness took place on a human scale. Her advice was: 'We can do no great things; only small things with great love.' She said to one man: 'If you can't feed 100 people then just feed one.' To another, who came asking what he could do for world peace, she responded 'Go home and love your family.'

Mother Teresa's work is not without controversy. It has been argued that she failed to raise people out of poverty, and had no long-term strategic goals. Perhaps these criteria simply don't apply to the role that Mother Teresa was born to play. Often her acts of kindness were very personal. In her Nobel Prize acceptance speech, she spoke about taking a woman from the streets and personally caring for her in the Home for the Dying in Kalighat until she passed away.

**'ONE KIND WORD CAN WARM THREE WINTER MONTHS'**
JAPANESE PROVERB

How can we explain the effect of Mother Teresa on the millions of people who never knew her, but who have been inspired by simply seeing her photograph or hearing about how she chose to live? She makes people feel happy. Seeing her image, they want to know more. She continues to bring people together in the name of kindness, and to reconnect them with a deep wish to put petty concerns aside and to dedicate oneself to the well-being of others.

## HOW DOES KINDNESS LEAD TO HAPPINESS?

At its most basic level, kindness is indispensable to the survival of living beings. From the very moment of our birth, we are dependent on the kindness of others. Even the most ferocious and savage animal starts life as a weak and defenceless creature, receiving food and shelter from another in order to survive. Later in life, we remain dependent on the kindness of countless other beings for our food, our shelter, our clothes, our medicines – the list is endless. What can we do to repay this kindness?

Kindness doesn't have to be soft and fuzzy. Wanting the best for someone else might involve speaking strongly, exerting discipline, or even firing them. The school teacher who gives out tough words with a loving attitude often has the most positive and lasting influence on our lives.

Many things can get in the way of kindness. It could be insecurity - the fear that someone will discover how little we know and how unsure we are of ourselves. Or distraction – when we're so busy running from one place to another that there's no time for anyone else. Or judgement – making decisions about what will be best

**TRUE STORY:** Abdul Aziz Said is an advisor and author on Middle East issues, Professor of International Relations and founder/director of the Centre for Global Peace at American University, Washington DC. He tells of his encounter with Bob, who once collected him from the airport to go to a conference. As they headed to the car, Bob disappeared, and Abdul found him helping an older woman with her luggage. A few moments later, as they walked on, he disappeared again. Intrigued, Abdul asked Bob what this was all about. Bob replied 'In the Vietnam war, I was part of a troop that checked for land mines. As we walked gingerly across a field, suddenly there would go my friend, Dave. A few steps more, and there would go another friend, Joe. I learned to notice things and take opportunities one step at a time.'

for someone else, instead of listening. Sometimes we waste our energy in debating whether to express kindness, instead of just getting on with it.

It is relatively easy to be kind to the people whom we like, and who are kind to us. However if we want to really make a difference in the world, we need to develop the capacity to be kind to the people beyond our comfort zone: to be polite to someone who is rude; to be helpful to someone who is unappreciative; to offer a gift to someone who rejects us. What does it take to care enough to do this?

**'WHAT WISDOM CAN YOU FIND THAT IS GREATER THAN KINDNESS?'** JEAN JACQUES ROUSSEAU, FRANCE

Being kind to ourselves is tricky territory. We may take great trouble to go after fun, comfort and beauty, but neglect to take care of our inner state – of what we need the most. Kindness involves sharing a tender place inside with others. How can we do that if we haven't paid attention to ourselves? We need to learn how to treat ourselves with loving kindness as well - to soften around our own pain and tread lightly around our fears.

When you take a moment to sit down, can you sit in peace? Or is your mind buzzing? Are your nerves jumbled? When you're with friends, can you be soft and receptive to them, while resting and relaxing deep within? If you can do this, laughter, humour and intimacy come more easily.

What is the key to developing kindness? First, we need to trust that, like everyone, we have the potential to be kind. We just have to learn how to access this kindness, how to find it inside and taste it for ourselves. One way to strengthen our motivation is simply to reflect, as often as we can, on the benefits that kindness brings. The tiny moments of satisfaction that come from caring for someone else, and from wanting them to be happy, can carry us through today, this year, this lifetime.

Kind people generally have more harmonious family lives, deeper friendships, more fun, and even better physical health. Kindness can be a powerful antidote to depression and low self-esteem because of its ability to take us out of self-absorption and to strengthen our connections with others.

For most people, it takes an effort to be constantly kind. We can watch and learn from those who are kind – how they listen and notice others' needs. Gradually we can stretch our own ability to be kind, until it becomes a habit.

**'IF YOU HAVEN'T ANY CHARITY IN YOUR HEART, YOU HAVE THE WORST KIND OF HEART TROUBLE'**
BOB HOPE, USA

It can be tempting to be casual about kindness, to treat it as a side issue of no real consequence. Yet here under our noses may be the whole secret to living a happy life. Cultivating the capacity to do something kind, which helps someone else feel happy, is often the most simple and straightforward route to our own happiness. What is stopping us from doing this?

**CHALLENGE:** Would you like to be more kind to other people? Or for them to be more kind to you? Take some extra time today to notice just one person. What are the little things that uplift or irritate them? What can you offer – a coffee, a conversation or just a smile? Respond in a way that is easy for them to receive. What difference did it make to your day?

## REFLECTION

- Find a quiet space where you can relax. Sit comfortably. To help you settle, focus your awareness on your breathing. Let go of any thoughts, images or feelings that arise. Whenever you become distracted, bring your awareness gently back to the sensation of the breath going in and out. Spend a few minutes enjoying the experience of coming to rest.

- Begin by generating a feeling of love and compassion towards yourself. 'May I be free of suffering.' Repeat these kind words over and over to yourself, either as a whisper or in silence. 'May I be free of suffering.'

- Recall the times when you have suffered in the past. Look at the ways that you are suffering at the moment. Whatever arises in your mind, gently respond with love and compassion. Continue to repeat 'May I be free of suffering.' Be very patient and soft towards yourself.

- Next, extend your love and compassion to the people or animals who you feel close to. Imagine compassion radiating out from your heart and gently washing away all their anxieties and difficulties, their suffering and pain. 'May they be free of suffering.'

- Extend your circle of love and compassion to include people and beings whom you have never met. You can focus on people in particular parts of the world or on those experiencing specific problems such as ill health or poverty or injustice. Or you can just think about all the people you don't know in your town or your country. Extend your love and compassion to every one of them without exception. 'May they be free of suffering.'

- Next, extend your love and compassion to the people whom you find challenging. Imagine them standing right here in front of you, and allow loving compassion to radiate out from your heart and gently wash away all their difficulties. 'May you be free of suffering.'

- Finally, imagine love and compassion spilling effortlessly out of your heart to embrace every living being in existence. Repeat gently 'May all beings be free from suffering.' Imagine these words radiating throughout the universe, vast and limitless. How does this make you feel?

- Close with the wish 'May all beings be happy!'

## RESOURCES

www.motherteresa.org is the official website of the Missionaries of Charity

Navin Chawla, Mother Teresa (London: Element Books, 1998).

Kathryn Spink, Mother Teresa: A Complete Authorized Biography (New York: HarperCollins, 1997).

'Mother Teresa: A Life of Devotion' 1989 (released on VHS by Vision Video, 1999).

**'MONEY IS A STICKY SUBSTANCE'**
MUHAMMAD YUNUS, BANGLADESH

# 06 HONESTY

## WHAT IS HONESTY?

Honesty is an opportunity to move through the world gracefully without harming other people. To speak or act dishonestly is to put our own interests ahead of someone else's. To distort what they experience to fit our needs, or to take their possessions for ourselves. This is why dishonesty causes such disappointment and pain. Whereas to be honest is to cherish the needs and wishes of someone else. It is a statement that we care about another person's welfare.

Honesty is a personal choice that arises every time that human beings connect with one another. Each individual has the opportunity to be straightforward and honest in their dealings with other people, regardless of their health, family situation, possessions or resources. In doing so, they help to create a culture of honesty for everyone.

Imagine a world where everyone plays fair, acts justly, and keeps their financial affairs simple and straightforward. Even the thought can make us soften and smile. It may take an enormous amount of courage and inner strength to bring this about, but why not get going right now? Honesty starts with each one of us.

## WHY MUHAMMAD YUNUS?

Nobel laureate Muhammad Yunus based the Grameen Bank of Bangladesh on a belief that people are fundamentally honest. He often states that it is not people who aren't credit-worthy – it is banks that aren't people-worthy. The aim of the bank is to lend money to impoverished people so that they can create a better life for themselves. 'Poverty does not belong in a civilized human society. It belongs in museums' declared Dr Yunus at the first World Micro-Credit Summit in 1997.

Yunus believes that every human being has unlimited potential. The policies and procedures of the Grameen Bank aim to develop that potential, particularly the quality of honesty. The bank requires no security against a loan, but employs a range of mechanisms to encourage repayment. Borrowers organise themselves into groups, payments are made in small weekly amounts and meetings take place under a village tree. The borrowers are shareholders in the bank. As a result, there is an extraordinarily low default rate – less than 1%.

Yunus says 'The meaning of the word 'credit' is trust. And yet over the years, as commercial banking has become institutionalised, it has built its entire edifice on the basis of mutual distrust.' Grameen has shown that there is another way. In 1998, after 22 years of business, it had over two million borrowers, 12,000 employees and 1,112 branches. However for Yunus 'our success is measured not by bad debt figures or repayment rates...but by whether the miserable and difficult lives of our borrowers have become less miserable, less difficult.'

> **'MONEY IS A GOOD SERVANT BUT A POOR MASTER'**
> TRADITIONAL SAYING

Jorimon is one such borrower, whose life has been transformed by the trust shown towards her by the Grameen Bank. 'Previously we went hungry for days on end; I worked like a slave in other people's houses; I walked from village to village with a heavy load of firewood on my head, trying to get some money in return. We had no home of our own. People used to ignore us all the time...But today God has shown us the path to happiness through the bank loan.'

## HOW DOES HONESTY LEAD TO HAPPINESS?

To have integrity – to act honestly, and be true to our word – is to trust that we can make our own way fairly in the world. But in looking after the interests of others and playing fair, we also take care of ourselves. Something deep inside can rest.

A good conscience is a pleasure and a relief. Integrity is a powerful antidote to strain and stress. We can look ourselves in the mirror, sleep easy, and derive contentment from the trust that others place in us.

> **'TO BUILD A WORLD OF JUSTICE, WE MUST BE JUST'**
> DAG HAMMARSKJOLD, SWEDEN

One of the most visible signals of our attitude towards honesty is the way in which we handle money. Despite the many aspects that money now takes, it is essentially a form of power, and one of the most fundamental ways in which human beings interact and connect with each other. To handle our finances in a fair way can be a source of quiet pleasure and of lasting self-respect.

To be dishonest around money and possessions is to forget how closely our own well-being depends upon our respect for the basic needs of others. Forgetting to pay a bus fare, taking stationery for our own use, or avoiding loan repayments

**TRUE STORY:** Biology professor and conservationist Pilai Poonswad is recruiting poachers and illegal loggers to her campaign to save the hornbills of South Thailand from extinction. 'Your children will dig up your bones and curse them for what you have done to the forests' she tells them. Pilai has successfully raised the money to protect more than 100 hornbill nests, set up a mobile learning centre with trained educators, and create alternative sources of employment and income for the local people. Ex-poachers now teach current poachers that regeneration will provide a safer future for them and their families rather than destruction and extermination. Pilai's dream is that these initiatives will foster more research into the complex web of life, and that modern Thais will rediscover what it means to live in harmony with the forest and with each other. In 2006 Pilai Poonswad was made a Laureate of the Rolex Awards for Enterprise for her visionary project.

Julian Cribb, Poachers into Gamekeepers, **www.sciencealert.com.au**, 28th June 2007.

may seem like matters of insignificance but, like air pollution, will soon come to harm a real person. Eventually the consequences will impact on us as well.

We all play different parts in the drama that is dishonesty. All of us know what it is to be cheated and lied to, and who hasn't exaggerated or been deceived by someone else? We continue to take the risk and pay the price even though it corrodes our relationships like acid. In a world saturated with material objects, there are hundreds of temptations to feed the fear that we don't have enough – power, money or charisma – and to reinforce the illusion we can take a short cut to happiness.

Dishonesty commonly feels secretive, yet it is often remarkably obvious when it is taking place. Somehow we intuit instinctively that we are being misled. Whether gross or subtle, we also know exactly when we ourselves are misleading people.

Betrayal brings shame and embarrassment. 'How could I have been so stupid or naïve?' 'Why did I trust that person?' The greater the trust and confidence in someone else, the harder and further we fall. The destructive cycle may even convince us that it is no longer worth behaving well ourselves. Once trust is broken, it can be impossible to repair. The fear of being found out will invariably increase, and the stakes can get very high.

'IN A TIME OF UNIVERSAL DECEIT, TELLING THE TRUTH BECOMES A REVOLUTIONARY ACT'
GEORGE ORWELL

So much of what goes on in the world depends on a distortion of reality. In a society fuelled by rampant competition it takes resilience and daring to remember that we may be able to get the job, partner and lifestyle that we hope for in a fair and open way. We rarely lose anything of real value through being honest. Nor does honesty need to be strident or blunt. It can be subtle, considered and refined.

There are countless reasons to tidy up our act and leave lying and cheating behind us. Whatever anyone has done, whatever anyone has said. There is always the option to let it go, to make amends, to pay back and to move beyond a pattern of living that is constrained by dishonesty. To move towards a way of life that rests with confidence on our integrity, on our most basic capacity to tell ourselves – and then others – the truth.

**CHALLENGE:** Is there anything that is niggling you? Is there a situation in which you have exaggerated or misrepresented yourself or your finances? Be honest with yourself so that you can be honest with somebody else.

## REFLECTION

- Find a quiet space where you can relax. Sit comfortably. To help you settle, focus your awareness on your breathing. Let go of any thoughts, images or feelings that arise. Whenever you become distracted, bring your awareness gently back to the sensation of the breath going in and out. Spend a few minutes enjoying the experience of coming to rest.

- Start by reflecting on the quality of honesty. Recall a situation where your honesty was put to the test and you managed to behave in a completely clean clear way; when you resisted the temptation to take something that wasn't really offered to you, or to twist the truth. How did it feel then? How does it feel now? Rejoice in your capacity to be honest and straightforward.

- Next, see if you can recall a situation when you failed to be as honest or straightforward as you would have liked. If some discomfort arises, notice it, identify it and persevere. Recall how you felt when you were not being honest, in as much detail as possible. Can you remember the sensation in your body?

- Reflect on the attitudes that lay behind your dishonest action. What led you to behave in this way? What did you hope to gain from it? Did it turn out the way you expected?

- Explore in your mind the implications of your behaviour. This may take some concentration and courage. How did your lack of honesty or transparency impact on other people? Will there have been a knock-on effect? What would happen if everyone behaved in this way?

- If you are feeling regret, can you turn this to good purpose? Can you redirect that self-critical energy and make a resolve to behave differently in the future? Visualise yourself as someone who is respected for their honesty and straightforwardness. Imagine yourself, in every instance, speaking truthfully and behaving with integrity. Enjoy the sensation of having a peaceful and clear conscience.

- Close with the wish 'May all beings be happy!'

## RESOURCES

www.muhammadyunus.org is the personal website of Muhammad Yunus and includes information and links relating to microfinance.

www.grameen-info.org is the website of the Grameen Bank, Bangladesh.

Mohammed Yunus with Alan Jolis, Banker to the Poor (Cambridge, MA: Public Affairs Books, 2003).

There are a range of videos about Muhammad Yunus and the Grameen Bank on the Bangladesh Video Archives site www.ethikana.com.

**'THE REAL WEALTH COMES FROM HELPING OTHERS'**
CÉSAR CHÁVEZ, MEXICO/USA

# 07 GENEROSITY

## WHAT IS GENEROSITY?

In some ways generosity seems a crazy, counter-cultural way to behave. Instead of keeping our time, energy or possessions for ourselves, we give them away. There is something very powerful about choosing to do this. It is a fundamental shift away from the limited world of 'me' and 'mine.'

Generosity is defined by the wish to benefit someone else. It is rarely the size of the gift or the gesture that matters most, but the message that comes with it. The heart knows this, immediately and unmistakeably. We taste the uneasiness when a gift has an ulterior motive, and save our real admiration for the person who can give without seeking a return.

To some degree, everyone on the planet is likely to demonstrate generosity in some way, whether to a member of their family, a friend, or a beloved animal. The question is simply whether we choose to go further than that. Whether we want to learn how to open our hearts and hands more widely, and to share more generously whatever time, energy, talents and possessions we have. It is a critical decision about the direction that we want our lives to take.

## WHY CÉSAR CHÁVEZ?

The Mexican/American farm worker, labour leader, and civil rights activist César Chávez was not in a position to demonstrate generosity through giving away money or possessions. He never earned more than 6,000 US dollars a year, didn't own a house, and left no savings to his family when he died. Nevertheless, more than 50,000 people attended his funeral in the small town of Delano, California to celebrate a lifetime of generosity that manifested through the gift of his time, talents, and energy to improve the working conditions of ordinary people in the USA. Chávez understood that 'the real wealth comes from helping others.'

As the son of migrant Mexican farm workers, Chávez watched as his parents were cheated of their land, and

'YOU HAVE NOT LIVED TODAY UNTIL YOU HAVE DONE SOMETHING FOR SOMEONE WHO CAN NEVER REPAY YOU'
JOHN BUNYAN, UK

his fellow workers were exploited by big landowners. He spoke later about how there grew in his heart 'a desire to be treated fairly, and to see my people treated as human beings and not as chattel. It grew from anger and rage, emotions I felt forty years ago when people of my color were denied the right to see a movie or eat at a restaurant in many parts of California. It grew from the frustration and humiliation I felt as a boy who couldn't understand how the growers could abuse and exploit farm workers when there were so many of us and so few of them.' He wanted to see more generosity in the world.

**'I EXPECT TO PASS THROUGH THIS WORLD BUT ONCE; ANY GOOD THING THEREFORE THAT I CAN DO, OR ANY KINDNESS THAT I CAN SHOW TO ANY FELLOW CREATURE, LET ME DO IT NOW; LET ME NOT DEFER OR NEGLECT IT, FOR I SHALL NOT PASS THIS WAY AGAIN'**
ETIENNE DE GRELLET, FRANCE

Taking St Francis of Assisi, Mahatma Gandhi and Martin Luther King Jr. as his inspiration, Chávez became a tireless campaigner for decent wages and working conditions. He co-founded an association which later became the United Farm Workers. He underwent month-long personal fasts to draw attention to issues such as the overuse of pesticides in US agriculture. He also became an early sponsor of Chicano art, and supported projects such as Il Teatro Campesino – The Farmworker's Theatre.

Chávez felt that 'the highest form of freedom carries with it the greatest measure of discipline.' He built his life on the principle that 'in this world it is possible to achieve great material wealth, to live an opulent life. But a life built upon those things alone leaves a shallow legacy. In the end, we will be judged by other standards.'

## HOW DOES GENEROSITY LEAD TO HAPPINESS?

Generosity is one of the most practical and straightforward methods that exists for bringing happiness into the world. It can happen at any time or place that people come together, it doesn't depend on intelligence and education, and it doesn't even require great wealth. Even the youngest member of the family knows instinctively how to cheer someone up with the gift of a hug, a flower, or a drawing they have done. It feels natural and good.

At its best, generosity is simply an outward sign of caring for the well-being of another person. A grandparent may give their time, a busy person can provide a useful contact, or a stranger will let us go first in the queue. What touches the heart and brings a lump to the throat is the love and kindness behind the gesture. Our warmest memories are often of times when people showed this kind of generosity to us, or when we ourselves were able to show generosity.

**TRUE STORY:** Mahadeb Mondal comes from a poor family in Chandkhali village, about 240km from Calcutta, India. At the age of eight years, he had to leave school and start earning money as a cowherd. His four labourer sons did the same. At the age of 70 years, he says 'Now I am old and infirm, I regret I could not study, or afford my sons' education. I wish I could put the clock back.' In May 2007 Mondal decided to do something that would help future generations of children in his village to get a better start in life. He gifted half his land to build a new primary school and continues to live in a thatched hut on the other half of the land with his wife Sabitri. The land gifted by Mondal is worth about 100,000 rupees, an extraordinary sum for someone who earns 40 rupees a day.

Reproduced with thanks from **The Telegraph**, Calcutta, 2 June 2007

In contrast, when we hold everything back for ourselves, our eyes narrow and our face goes tight. The more we store things up, the more we fear their loss. Joy is not to be found in being miserly, but in doing something that makes a child's face light up, that draws a reluctant grin from an adolescent, or touches an older person's heart. Unless we're in the worst of moods, the smile we bring to someone else's face will quickly spread to our own.

In low moments, when our heart has closed down, we may feel we have nothing to give. Yet we can always offer a friendly word, an understanding glance or a companionable silence, and we may find this is the very medicine that will lift us out of our own loneliness and sadness. It is sometimes only through being generous that we discover our own wealth and value.

Generosity can help us to establish a right relationship with our possessions. Are they really 'ours,' or simply a form of loan from the universe, which may not even last a lifetime? Do we make good use of them, or would they be of more benefit to someone else? It can be a relief to loosen our grip, and to let objects and energy move around in a more relaxed and open way. It can encourage us to re-examine what we think we need, and taste the subtle pleasure of letting go.

**'YOU MAKE A LIVING BY WHAT YOU GET. YOU MAKE A LIFE BY WHAT YOU GIVE'**
WINSTON CHURCHILL, UK

Generosity can also help us to move beyond a self-interested fixation with 'me, me, me.' To give away something we don't want is hardly generosity at all. To give away something that we enjoy and use – or had a future use for – is a potentially radical way of putting someone else's interests first. Once we have discovered this unique satisfaction, it may become a habit.

**'WE SHOULD GIVE AS WE WOULD RECEIVE, CHEERFULLY, QUICKLY, AND WITHOUT HESITATION; FOR THERE IS NO GRACE IN A BENEFIT THAT STICKS TO THE FINGERS'**
SENECA, ANCIENT ROME

However it is possible to lose the essence of generosity by twisting it to our own purposes and practising it with a mixed motivation. To what extent are we chasing rewards? Do we use generosity as a way to gain power and influence? What draws us to over-extend ourselves, and offer something that is beyond our means and will throw us off balance? The most flamboyant gifts sometimes come with a hidden price tag. To give well and sincerely, it is important to use our wisdom and keep our feet on the ground.

If giving feels good, it makes sense that skilfully extending our capacity to give can make us feel even better. The opportunities to do this are never-ending. Can we let someone else take the last parking place, give up our place in the queue to a stranger, or spend the lunch hour with a new colleague? It can be revealing to ask ourselves how readily we will let someone else have their own way, even at our expense, and how far we will go to be generous to the people that we dislike.

It is always possible to deepen our practice of generosity. To refine our motivation to give, to rejoice in the giving itself and to derive satisfaction from the fact that we have given. It is a lifetime's practice.

**CHALLENGE:** Could you be giving more to others than you do at the moment? In what area would that be – your time, your skills or your resources? Are you willing to engage beyond your normal comfort zone? Commit to something now.

## REFLECTION

- Find a quiet space where you can relax. Sit comfortably. To help you settle, focus your awareness on your breathing. Let go of any thoughts, images or feelings that arise. Whenever you become distracted, bring your awareness gently back to the sensation of the breath going in and out. Spend a few minutes enjoying the experience of coming to rest.

- Let your imagination take you to your favourite room in your home – the cosiest and most comfortable place where you most like to spend your time. Settle yourself down in the place where you normally like to be. Take a deep breath and relax.

- Take a leisurely look around the room. Pass your gaze over all the objects that it contains. Then focus in turn on all the objects that you received as a gift. Each one will carry its own memory. Can you take your mind back to the moment of the gift, and the expression of the person who gave it to you? Why did they give it to you? How did you feel at the time?

- Next, focus on all the objects in the room that you purchased for yourself. Each one will have its own individual history. Where did it come from? What is it made of? Who might have grown, woven, hammered, printed, designed, assembled or carved the object for your eventual use? How many people were involved in its packaging and transportation? Stretch your mind as far and wide as possible, to encompass all the beings who helped to bring this object into your possession.

- Do you own anything that you did not receive through the generosity of another person? Survey the room and try to find one single thing that is there without the involvement of anyone else.

- Consider the idea that it is only through the kindness of others that we enjoy possessions, sustenance, and nurture. What are the invisible connections between us that enable us to keep each other alive? What are the effects of the thoughtless and unskilful actions we are also caught up in, such as taking more than we need?

- From the comfort of your favourite room, reflect on how you would like to behave towards other beings. Is there something you can do to repay their kindness?

- Close with the wish "May all beings be happy!"

## RESOURCES

www.chavezfoundation.org is the website of the César E Chávez Foundation, which aims 'to maximise human potential to improve our communities'.

Susan Ferriss and Ricardo Sandoval, The Fight in the Fields: César Chávez and the Farmworkers' Movement (Harvest/HBJ, Paperback Edition 1998).

'The Fight in the Fields: César Chávez and the Farmworkers' Struggle' directed by Rick Tejada-Flores and Ray Telles, 1997 (originally produced by Paradigm Productions, and available on VHS from The Cinema Guild Inc, New York).

**'IT DOES NOT TAKE MANY WORDS TO SPEAK THE TRUTH'**
CHIEF JOSEPH, NEZ PERCE FIRST NATION

# 08 RIGHT SPEECH

## WHAT IS RIGHT SPEECH?

Words! Love them or hate them, it often feels like we're drowning in the noise they create – not only in our own ears, or on the page, but in our heads. They have the power to uplift us and to cast us down, to liberate and to entrap. They create friendships and make enemies. They can gain us great wealth and lose us everything we possess. The power of speech is so great that words cannot do it justice.

As soon as a child learns to speak, its life and relationships change. Countless daily choices come next. Whether to speak loudly or quietly, fast or slow. What words to use. When to speak or to be silent. We learn how to use our speech through trial and error, and in doing so create an image and style that will define our personality and shape our lives.

**'DEATH AND LIFE ARE IN THE POWER OF THE TONGUE'**
KING SOLOMON

Right speech is a commitment to use words skilfully, in a way that will bring peace and happiness to ourselves and the people around us. It is about using our speech to take away fear, to bring hope, to make people laugh and feel closer to one another. This is how we share who we are and what is in our heart.

## WHY CHIEF JOSEPH?

'Chief Joseph' was born in 1840 in what is now Oregon, USA. He was elected leader of the Nez Perce at a time when his first nation was struggling to resist the takeover of its homeland by American colonists. His surrender speech of October 1877, given after a 1400 mile march, immortalised him as a voice of conscience in American popular culture.

Truthful words and honourable behaviour are of utmost importance to Native Americans because they form the bedrock of society and trade. Chief Joseph said of Lewis and Clark, the first colonists that he encountered: 'They talked straight and our people gave them a great feast as proof that their hearts were friendly.' Tragically, this positive first impression left the Nez Perce vulnerable to the lies and betrayals that followed.

Chief Joseph was confused and dismayed at the way other colonists behaved. When he visited Washington in 1879, he said: 'I cannot understand how the Government sends a man out to fight us, as it did General Miles, and then breaks his word. Such a government has something wrong about it. I cannot understand why so many chiefs are allowed to talk so many different ways, and promise so many different things... I am tired of talk that comes to nothing. It makes my heart sick when I remember all the good words and all the broken promises'.

'IT IS ONLY IN THE DEPTHS OF SILENCE THAT THE VOICE OF GOD CAN BE HEARD' SAI BABA, INDIA

'Good words do not last long unless they amount to something. Words do not pay for my dead people. They do not pay for my country now overrun by white men.'

## HOW DOES RIGHT SPEECH LEAD TO HAPPINESS?

Right speech is the natural consequence of genuinely caring for another person and wanting to contribute to their well-being. It does not set out to harm or knowingly deceive, and it avoids turning people against each other. There is enormous satisfaction in knowing that we have spoken truthfully and well. Our breathing is regular. Our body and mind are at peace.

Right speech takes place all around us, sometimes in the most unexpected ways. It might be the boss at work who instinctively knows when a sincere word of praise will make all the difference. It may be the colleague who notices that something is worrying us and writes a sympathetic note. It is often the receptionist who has learned the art of offering a warm welcome to hundreds of people a day. It's such a relief when someone speaks to us in a manner that relates to how we feel or what we need to know.

'NOISE PROVES NOTHING. OFTEN THE HEN WHO HAS MERELY LAID AN EGG CACKLES AS IF SHE HAD LAID AN ASTEROID' MARK TWAIN, USA

It is often the softly spoken word that makes its point, and the gentlest voice to which people pay most attention. However, right speech is not always quiet. We may be called to say exactly what is needed at a public meeting, or to stand up calmly but with force to a colleague who has confronted us at work. Stern yet skilful words may be necessary to discipline a child, or to be honest and direct with a friend.

It can be very revealing to look at what we say and write. Are we somebody who commonly complains or criticises others? Do we swiftly offer our opinion, even

**TRUE STORY:** Buckminster Fuller was an American visionary who invented the geodesic dome and was an early advocate for solar power. However at the age of 32, he was on the verge of a breakdown. His first child had died. He had a wife and new-born baby but was bankrupt, discredited and jobless. Contemplating suicide on the shores of Lake Michigan, it suddenly struck him that his life belonged, not to himself, but to the universe. At that moment he chose to embark on an experiment to discover what a single penniless and unknown individual could do for humanity. He vowed not to speak until his every thought and word would be helpful to others. His silence lasted for two years but led to a period of intensive altruistic creativity. In time, Buckminster Fuller left behind a legacy of inventions and earned himself the epithet 'the grandfather of the future.'

when it is only half-formed? How often do we spread gossip or scandal, spilling secrets that are not ours to share? Do we exaggerate, to make ourselves seem more important or exciting than we really are? Our speech betrays more about us than we might wish.

> **'IT IS ONLY IN THE DEPTHS OF SILENCE THAT THE VOICE OF GOD CAN BE HEARD' SAI BABA, INDIA**

Right speech is a world apart from the noisy, whirling words that dramatize and misrepresent, or the 'half listening' that we do when we are feeling tired, rushed or plain competitive. It is very different from the non-stop chatter that exhausts and distracts. The more we talk, or get talked to, the less chance there is that we will use our speech in a meaningful way. Speech can easily become draining rather than uplifting.

Sometimes the most beneficial course of action is to remain silent. To hold back the comment that makes the conversation fly faster but makes people feel uneasy. To resist making a joke that raises a cheap laugh but leaves someone hurting inside. To refrain from writing the email that shares some information that is better kept private.

It is an act of great kindness to develop the ability to be quiet in someone else's company, to gently explore how our presence can be most helpful. Do we have the strength to listen deeply

> **'STICKS AND STONES MAY BREAK MY BONES, BUT WORDS WILL MAKE ME GO IN A CORNER AND CRY BY MYSELF FOR HOURS' ERIC IDLE, UK**

and offer another person the space to say anything they want? Can we make ourselves available to a grieving friend and, leaving our own opinions on one side, simply reflect back to them what they already know? When we do this, the barriers between the other person and ourselves can fade away.

Such stillness is not learned in an instant. It comes from within, as the expression of a calm and balanced mind. If we are at peace with ourselves, with nothing to disguise or prove, then our speech is more likely to be pleasing and appropriate. When we are genuinely focused on what the other person needs from us, rather than anything we want from them, then our speech will naturally be more constructive, kind and helpful.

Those who are wise and compassionate know instinctively what to say. Their own lightness, joy and passion tumble spontaneously through the way they talk and laugh, and carry the power to shift the listener beyond habitual pain and problems. Their speech and writing become tools to inspire and uplift – to bring more happiness into the world. What a difference it will make if we can do the same.

**CHALLENGE:** When is the last time you said something that made you cringe? For the space of one hour, can you take care over every word that you say? Can you speak only words that contribute to the welfare of the person you are talking to? Listen deeply to discover what those words need to be.

## REFLECTION

- Find a quiet space where you can relax. Sit comfortably. To help you settle, focus your awareness on your breathing. Let go of any thoughts, images or feelings that arise. Whenever you become distracted, bring your awareness gently back to the sensation of the breath going in and out. Spend a few minutes enjoying the experience of coming to rest.

- What does 'right speech' mean for you? Think of a time when you watched someone speak with kindness, sensitivity and wisdom. How did it feel? What did it sound like? What effect did it have on the people around them?

- Reflect on some of the conversations that you have had today – their content, their tone and their purpose. Would you describe them as right speech?

- Bring to mind a recent occasion when you gossiped about someone else, or criticised them behind their back. This may be difficult or uncomfortable. Try to recall this conversation without judging yourself or the listener.

- Be gentle but probing. What were you doing at the time? What motivated you to speak in this way? How did it make you feel? What effect did it have on other people?

- Next visualise that you walk into a room where two people are talking about you. They don't see you, but you overhear them gossiping and criticising. Imagine that this is really happening and watch how you react. What happens to your body? What happens in your mind? How do you feel towards them? What will you do next?

- If this imaginary gossip and criticism has hurt you, then treat yourself with great kindness and gentleness. Acknowledge that you are experiencing pain without seeking to blame the people concerned.

- Try to extend the same kindness and gentleness to the person whom you have hurt with your own criticism and gossip. Is there a way for you to make amends? What is holding you back from doing this? What would it take to use your speech more wisely in the future?

- Close with the wish 'May all beings be happy!'

## RESOURCES

www.nezperce.org is the official website of the Nez Perce Tribe and provides information on its tribal government, programs and departments, history, celebrations, businesses, and reservation.

Kent Nerburn, Chief Joseph and the Flight of the Nez Perce: The Untold Story of an American Tragedy (New York: HarperOne, 2005).

Robert Penn Warren, Chief Joseph of the Nez Perce (New York: Random House, 1983) is a narrative poem inspired by Chief Joseph.

Chief Joseph is featured in the PBS series New Perspectives on the West www.pbs.org/weta/thewest which includes a range of classroom resources.

# HOW WE RELATE TO OTHERS

# Cherish others: independence is a myth

It is a simple fact, whether we like it or not, that we cannot get by on our own. Take a look at the act of eating breakfast. Half-asleep, or in a rush to get to work on time, it is easy to forget the people behind the scenes who make your existence possible. Whether it is the farmer who grew the seed for your bread, the engineer who brought the water for your tea, or the van driver who supplied the shop: your connections with others are endless. If you pursue the matter to its logical conclusion, you will find that you are linked to every being on the planet, past, present and future.

Our tendency to overlook or ignore these infinite connections is not only unrealistic, but a major obstacle to happiness. There is a deep rooted inclination to see ourselves as separate individuals who have worked hard to be 'self-sufficient' and 'independent'. Advertising slogans give the message that it is ok to be self-centred, to 'look after No.1' and to prioritise our own needs and concerns. At school or at work, on the TV and in the newspapers, we are encouraged to compete rather than to collaborate. The result is often isolation, loneliness, anxiety and depression.

It does not take much effort to see that the happiest people we know are those who acknowledge their interdependence, and who nurture warm and appreciative relationships with the people around them. On a day-to-day basis, this is probably the most immediate cause of happiness or suffering for any human being. Nobody likes to be criticised or disliked – the sour taste of disapproval can linger for days or even years. In contrast, someone who is a genuine source of support and encouragement for the people around them is never short of friends. To be kind to others is a kindness to yourself.

At the root of the strongest and most lasting relationships is a sincere wish for the other person to be happy. Cultivating this thought sets in motion a chain of events in which you naturally learn to act with more warmth and kindness, and they in turn are more likely to respond positively towards you. Even when you get it wrong and behave unskilfully, the fact that you did not intend to hurt will often soothe the situation.

The four qualities of respect, forgiveness, gratitude and loyalty are a powerful tool to strengthen our relationships with the people around us. Since our own happiness ultimately depends on theirs, this is one of the most direct and effective routes to a happy life.

'A HUNDRED TIMES EVERY DAY I REMIND MYSELF THAT MY INNER AND OUTER LIFE ARE
BASED ON THE LABOURS OF OTHER MEN, LIVING AND DEAD'
ALBERT EINSTEIN, GERMANY/USA

# 09 RESPECT

## WHAT IS RESPECT?

Everyone wants and needs respect. It is a pre-requisite for human beings to relate to each other in a positive and constructive way. Respect acknowledges that we have the same basic needs, whether physical, psychological or spiritual, and that other people's experience and wisdom can be helpful to us.

Yet there is another dimension to respect, with even more power to transform. From our earliest years, we learn and grow through admiring and copying other people. In traditional societies this was and is a well-ordered process. Wisdom and life experience are seen as a form of wealth to be passed down the generations. 'Elder' does not just mean 'old.' Why is there now often a tendency to be disrespectful towards people who are older and have more life experience than ourselves?

All around us there are people we can respect and learn from, if we choose to do so, and if we have the necessary humility. Respect is something that we have to give rather than to demand. How do we choose the people we respect? What effect will this have on our lives? How can respect contribute to a happy life?

## WHY ALBERT EINSTEIN?

Albert Einstein wrestled with the issue of respect all through his life. 'Long live impudence! It is my guardian angel in this world!' he famously declared. His scientific discoveries were driven by an extraordinary ability to question. 'I have no special talents. I am only passionately curious.' At the same time he was capable of innate humility. Even when he was one of the most famous scientists in the world, he still described himself as a curious child standing before the great mystery of the universe.

Einstein's own investigation into the nature of the universe convinced him that human beings are interdependent rather than independent. 'When we survey our lives and endeavours we soon observe that almost the whole of our actions and desires are bound up with the existence of other human beings' he said. On this basis he tried to be a dutiful son to his parents, even when they opposed his marriage. 'We mustn't forget that many existences like my parents' make our existence possible' he reminded his future wife – and himself.

Einstein believed that to develop respect for people with more knowledge or understanding than ourselves is a vital part of human development. When he was living in the USA, he was invited to share his views on education by the New York State Education Department. 'In teaching history,' he replied 'there should be extensive discussion of personalities who benefited mankind through independence of character and judgement.'

In keeping with his views, Einstein treated his scientific heroes with enormous reverence. However he was capable of being flamboyantly disrespectful to the teachers he didn't respect. 'Let every man be respected as an individual and no man idolised' he said. Although Einstein was capable of profound respect, it had to be based on thinking for oneself. He stated on many occasions that blind respect for authority is the greatest enemy of truth. Perhaps it was this combination of respect and free thinking that powered his greatest achievements as a scientific and humanitarian thinker.

## HOW DOES RESPECT LEAD TO HAPPINESS?

Giving and receiving respect feels good. It warms the heart and lifts the spirits. 'I like this person. I respect the way they carry themselves, what they say, how they behave.' Words are often unnecessary. We know intuitively whether or not we respect someone, and whether we are respected by them.

In contrast, disrespect is a painful expression of not paying attention to another person's achievements or needs. Instead of closeness and warmth, disrespect creates loneliness and isolation. We know when it is happening. The joke is against us. Two colleagues exchange a knowing smile. We get left out of an important meeting. Our heart sinks and our confidence ebbs away. We start looking over our shoulder. It's a lonely place to be.

When someone shows respect to us, they affirm who we are and how we choose to live. Nothing showy or glamorous needs to take place. We can respect someone for speaking just one sentence – or for staying silent. We can respect the person who cleans the floor of a board room just as much – or more than - the person who sits in a big chair and signs the cheques.

Genuine respect comes from the heart and is freely given. It isn't a measure of worldly achievement. The university professor who constantly tells people how many books he has written is often undermining his credibility. The military

**TRUE STORY:** In 1981, a housewife called Barbara Wiedner became aware that there were 150 nuclear weapons ready for firing at an air force base near her home in Sacramento, California. She was struck by the fact that 'if things did not change, my precious grandchildren could be part of the last generation on earth' and joined the protestors with a sign (made by one of her grand-daughters) that read 'Grandmother for Peace.' The following year, during her first spell in jail for non-violent civil disobedience, Barbara decided to link up with other grandparents to capitalise on their unique voice and role in society. Grandmothers for Peace is now an international network of volunteers who campaign on 'peace and justice issues that affect the human family' such as the danger of nuclear power plants, radioactive waste, the weaponisation of space, and global militarism. They also offer Peace & Justice Scholarship Awards, and commit to guide their grandchildren in the ways of non-violence. Barbara commented that 'In most cultures around the world, grandmothers are revered as the 'keepers of the peace'. We are inspired and motivated by that fact, but realize that in today's dangerous world we can no longer keep or promote peace by sitting in our rocking chairs.' Barbara passed away in December 2001 but the organisation that she founded continues to flourish.

Taken with permission from **www.grandmothersforpeace.org**

leader who demands respect through impressive uniforms and extravagant ceremonies, big statues or elaborate town planning is seeking to build respect on poor foundations.

If respect is to be truly beneficial, it needs to be grounded in wisdom and discernment. We need to check up carefully. How happy are the people that we choose to respect? Do they possess the qualities and principles that we most want to acquire? Children spend a huge amount of time mimicking and dreaming about the attributes of their heroes, wishing they had their good looks, their skills, their wealth or their intelligence. Our lives are shaped by the people we choose to respect.

'THE HERO IS ONE WHO KINDLES A GREAT LIGHT IN THE WORLD, WHO SETS UP BLAZING TORCHES IN THE DARK STREETS OF LIFE FOR MEN TO SEE BY'
FELIX ADLER, USA

The strength and energy to go beyond our usual limits often comes from being inspired by someone who has travelled further along the path and is calling out to us. All the people featured in this book have this special potential to inspire. Whether we are held by the straight gaze of Aung San Suu Kyi, or compelled by the playful genius of Albert Einstein, we admire their special qualities and want to be more like them.

'How conceited to think that I could be like that – it's impossible' is the thought that holds us back. 'How can I understand and learn from them?' is the thought that takes us forward. Somehow we need to create a relationship with the people we admire that picks us up, not puts us down. This is the shadow side to respect – when it turns into a kind of laziness, an admission of defeat or even envy. 'I'll never make the grade.'

Is there something to be learnt about respect from the world of sport? An athlete who wants to excel will seek out a coach or mentor whom they have reason to respect. Perhaps someone who has already succeeded, and knows what needs to be done. Someone who has the patience and the perseverance to stay with their students through all the ups and downs. Who is unselfish enough to take pleasure in what their students achieve. It is a well-tested recipe for excellence and achievement.

**'THERE IS NO MAN SO BAD, BUT HE SECRETLY RESPECTS THE GOOD' BENJAMIN FRANKLIN, USA**

There is a traditional Indian story called the 'Four Harmonious Friends' that illustrates the importance of all the diverse elements in society respecting each other and working together for the common good. It describes an elephant (the elder), a monkey, a rabbit, and a bird, who all live together in a beautiful forest. They discover that without respect and co-operation, they cannot get the food they need. The story is often illustrated by a picture of the four animals standing on each other to reach a succulent fruit that is hanging from a tree. By respecting each other's qualities, they can live in harmony and bring prosperity to the whole community.

**CHALLENGE:** If you had to choose one role model for your life, who would it be? Which of their strengths do you yearn to have? Which strengths do you have in common? What is your particular way of expressing these strengths? During the next week, notice and rejoice every time you put them to good use, and remember the person who has inspired you.

## REFLECTION

● Find a quiet space where you can relax. Sit comfortably. To help you settle, focus your awareness on your breathing. Let go of any thoughts, images or feelings that arise. Whenever you become distracted, bring your awareness gently back to the sensation of the breath going in and out. Spend a few minutes enjoying the sensation of coming to rest.

- Cast your mind back over the stories you have read in this book. Reflect on what it is that draws you to them. Is there one person who particularly inspires you? Alternatively, focus on someone who is not in the book and who you know personally. In either case, think about the very specific qualities that you respect in that person.

- Consider which qualities of this person you would most like to develop within yourself. Are they qualities that you already possess? Remember a time when, even on a smaller scale, you demonstrated some of these qualities in the way you thought, spoke or behaved. What do you already have in common with them?

- Now imagine this person, to whom you look up, as a baby, and then as a small child. Reflect on how they had to learn to speak, walk, read and write, just as you did. Reflect on the moments in the middle of the night when they may have felt uncertain and afraid. What mistakes do you think they made? How did they cope with their mistakes?

- Try to accept the vulnerability and humanity of this person you respect. They are a human being, just like you. Spend some time focusing on their vulnerability. Does it make any difference to the quality of your respect?

- Is there any reason that you cannot develop the same qualities that you admire in others? Can you transcend your own limitations, including your limited view of yourself?

- Allow yourself to 'think big' for a few minutes, just as they may have done.

- Close with the wish 'May all beings be happy!'

## RESOURCES

www.alberteinstein.info provides online access to the scientific and non-scientific manuscripts held by the Albert Einstein Archives at the Hebrew University of Jerusalem and to an extensive Archival Database.

Albert Einstein, The World as I See It (New York: Citadel Press, 2007).

Walter Isaacson, Einstein – His Life and Universe (London: Simon & Schuster, 2007).

Abraham Pais, Subtle Is the Lord: The Science and the Life of Albert Einstein (Oxford: Oxford University Press, 2005) provides an overview of Einstein's scientific thought.

There is an online exhibition about Albert Einstein on the website of the American Museum of Natural History www.amnh.org/exhibitions/einstein.

'TO FORGIVE IS NOT JUST TO BE ALTRUISTIC. IT IS THE BEST FORM OF SELF-INTEREST'
DESMOND TUTU, SOUTH AFRICA

# 10 FORGIVENESS

## WHAT IS FORGIVENESS?

Forgiveness is the capacity to reclaim our peace of mind when something has happened to disturb us. As we go through life it is inevitable that we are going to hurt one another. In fact, as our world becomes more complex and interconnected, the opportunities for conflict increase. We have the choice whether to respond to these hurts and conflicts with anger and bitterness, or with forgiveness.

Forgiving is not the same as forgetting. It does not mean that we gloss over the harm that has taken place, or pretend that it never happened. What it does is to allow us to let go of the destructive attitudes towards the past that imprison us and the person who harmed us in a cycle of recrimination and guilt. When our desire for reconciliation and peace is stronger than our anger, disappointment or pain, then forgiveness offers the opportunity to make a new start.

Forgiveness can seem insurmountable, and has vast consequences, but in essence it is nothing more than a shift of mind. The motivation to forgive has to come from a genuine wish deep inside to relieve the pain and discomfort of ourselves and of others. It cannot be forced. Does everyone have the capacity to forgive? Can everything be forgiven? Is forgiveness something we can learn?

## WHY DESMOND TUTU?

When Desmond Tutu speaks about forgiveness, he often tells the story of the young anti-apartheid activist Malusi Mpumlwana who was detained without trial in prison and tortured by the South African security police during the late 1970s and early 1980s. One of the ways that Malusi coped with his brutal treatment was to remember that although the police were behaving inhumanely, they were also God's children and depended on him to recover the humanity they had lost.

The Truth and Reconciliation Commission, set up in 1995 to promote restorative rather than retributive justice in the new South Africa, was grounded in the same philosophy: that we are all are interconnected and depend on each other to learn and grow. As the Chair of the Commission, Tutu listened to harrowing testimonies that moved him to tears. Nevertheless, he maintained his belief that everyone has the potential for forgiveness and reconciliation. 'Yes indeed these people were guilty of monstrous, even diabolical deeds [but] that did not turn them into monsters or demons.'

Tutu is a down to earth man. He speaks of his own struggle to say 'sorry' to his wife, even in the intimacy and love of their bedroom. In his analysis, everyone makes mistakes, and the starting point is to admit this. Sorrow or contrition lead to confession, to forgiveness and finally to reconciliation. He is adamant you cannot ignore the wrong, or brush it under the carpet. He says: 'If you are neutral in situations of injustice, you have chosen the side of the oppressor. If an elephant has its foot on the tail of a mouse and you say that you are neutral, the mouse will not appreciate your neutrality.'

**'ONLY THE BRAVE KNOW HOW TO FORGIVE' LAURENCE STERNE, IRELAND**

In some ways, Desmond Tutu might seem an unlikely personality to win a Nobel Prize for Peace. He is often outspoken and provocative, and has had lively public quarrels with other South African leaders such as Thabo Mbeki and even Nelson Mandela. Like the Old Testament prophet Jeremiah, he feels no choice but to speak his mind. Yet it is his openness and vulnerability that strengthen his power to connect with people, and encourage them to develop their own capacity to forgive. With his broad smile and infectious giggle, he has now travelled all over the world as an ambassador for forgiveness.

## HOW DOES FORGIVENESS LEAD TO HAPPINESS?

Forgiveness celebrates our special capacity to love and reach out to someone else, whatever has happened between us. The more we forgive, the more we experience the benefits it brings. Joy comes back into the house. We sleep better. We get our energy back. Everyone feels lighter and happier. New levels of understanding, creativity and intimacy arise.

It is a triumph of the human spirit when people choose kindness and harmony over bitterness and conflict. When they manage to overcome their anger, and to speak with or even extend a hand of friendship to the person who hurt them. It is a cause for admiration and celebration. 'Did that person really manage to forgive? Despite everything they went through?'

To forgive is to acknowledge that life is in flux. Human relationships are complex and constantly changing. The drama we experience is only part of the picture, one piece of the jigsaw. Forgiveness admits that there is a wider perspective, which we may not be able to see for ourselves.

**TRUE STORY:** Anne Gallagher is a former nurse from Belfast who looked after victims of bombs and bullets on both sides of the sectarian divide. 'Seeing them lying there, naked and attached to life support machines, I didn't see a uniform, I just saw their hearts, their pain.' She also experienced The Troubles first hand. Her father and three brothers were interned without trial, and her brother Dominic was shot dead in front of his young son. Her response was to set up Seeds of Hope, an organisation that facilitates story telling, based on The Troubles, through music, art, drama, writing and sport. 'We listen to people's stories, but we don't judge them. There's healing in that. The idea is that when you hear my story and I hear your story, it becomes our story, and seeds of hope are sown.' Similar work is now being carried out in prisons, schools and communities in Sweden, Belgium and the USA.

Reproduced with permission from The Forgiveness Project **www.theforgivenessproject.com**

It is so painful to carry a grudge. To water the seeds of our anger and continue to dwell in the pain of a real or imagined wrong. The suffering that we neglect can lead to generations of unhappy relations. Simply becoming aware of its poisonous power can help us find the motivation to seek relief.

To forgive small hurts is part of daily life. The person who can do this well has a special calm and warmth about them. We admire a forgiving person, and wonder what their secret is. Heroic stories of people who have forgiven a major betrayal, a violation or a tragedy can restore our faith in human nature and put our own dramas into perspective. They can inspire us to re-examine our attitudes to forgiveness and to acknowledge its complexity, and its possibility.

Every time we manage to forgive makes it a little bit easier the next time around. It is reassuring that we can do it, however confused and vulnerable we feel. We may surprise ourselves, and gain the confidence to deal with fresh and perhaps greater hurts. 'I managed to forgive that...so now I can forgive this.' How can we make this into a habit?

The key to forgiveness is giving – what we value, the best we can do. And the main commitment is to pay attention – first to ourselves, and then to the person or situation that we feel has harmed us. It is an act of generosity and surrender to

'O LORD, REMEMBER NOT ONLY THE MEN AND WOMEN OF GOOD WILL, BUT ALL THOSE OF ILL WILL. BUT DO NOT REMEMBER ALL THE SUFFERING THEY HAVE INFLICTED UPON US. REMEMBER THE FRUITS WE HAVE BROUGHT THANKS TO THIS SUFFERING – OUR COMRADESHIP, OUR LOYALTY, OUR HUMILITY, OUR COURAGE, OUR GENEROSITY, THIS GREATNESS OF HEART WHICH HAS GROWN OUT OF ALL THIS. AND WHEN THEY COME TO JUDGEMENT, LET ALL THE FRUITS WE HAVE BORNE BE THEIR FORGIVENESS'

FOUND IN RAVENSBRÜCK CONCENTRATION CAMP IN 1945

suspend our judgements and preoccupations, and to listen closely to another person's story. To put all our energy and attention into this process, and not be distracted by the cynical dimension of our own mind.

It is unlikely we will find the necessary clarity and kindness to forgive if we remain unforgiving, fearful or defensive towards ourselves. What does it take to turn our attention gently inwards and to acknowledge the unskilful things we have said and done, the pain we have caused, and the ways in which we don't live up to our own standards? Everyone makes mistakes – it is part of life and the only way to learn. Yet it demands great courage, and sometimes the help of another person, to admit our vulnerability and hurt.

Can forgiveness and apology take place without facing up to the person who either harmed us or bore the impact of our own unskilful behaviour? It may make sense to hold back from dealing directly with the person or institution that hurt us. When the real work has taken place, inside us, in private, then we can decide whether an outer show of reconciliation is necessary or helpful.

Forgiveness can work its magic years after the event. If the moment has passed and the people moved on, then it is only our own thoughts and feelings that keep us in an unforgiving place. If we can find the courage to go beyond that place, the benefit is all ours. The feeling can be amazing – like stepping out blinking into bright sunlight. What does it take to make this happen?

**CHALLENGE:** Which person has the most power to make you irritated and upset? How much time do you spend thinking about them? Check up. Do you get upset when this person fails to meet your own expectations or needs? Are your expectations realistic? Can you create some space in your mind in which forgiveness can take root. Can it help you be less angry next time around?

## REFLECTION

● Find a quiet space where you can relax. Sit comfortably. To help you settle, focus your awareness on your breathing. Let go of any thoughts, images or feelings that arise. Whenever you become distracted, bring your awareness gently back to the sensation of the breath going in and out. Spend a few minutes enjoying the sensation of coming to rest.

- Imagine that as you breathe in, you are inhaling blissful light. It is white, the colour of purity. The light represents all the positive qualities that exist in the universe. It represents all the qualities of the people you admire, and which you would like to develop within yourself.

- As you breathe in this light, imagine it flowing through the whole of your body. All the way to your toes and finger tips. Filling every tiny space of your body, down to the cells, the atoms and the subatomic particles.

- Spend some time breathing in the white light, letting it fill your whole body. Imagine that it has the capacity to heal whatever anxieties, problems, pain and sicknesses you are carrying in your body and mind.

- Generate a conviction that this is really happening, that this blissful clear light is actually entering your body and filling every crevice. Your body becomes very light and transparent and relaxed.

- Now begin to imagine dark smoke or pollution coming out of your body when you exhale. This smoke represents all the times that you have been angry with yourself. When you have said something that you regret or that didn't feel right.

- Every time you breathe out, let this anger and pain leave your body, in the form of dark smoke. Watch it disappear into space. It doesn't pollute or disturb anything, it just disappears into space.

- Continue for as long as you can, imagining the white light coming in and the dark smoke going out. Forgive yourself. Enjoy the sensation of the body and mind becoming blissful and clean clear, free of all problems and negativities.

- Close with the wish 'May all beings be happy!'

## RESOURCES

www.tutu.org is the website of The Desmond Tutu Peace Centre, which aims to nurture peace by promoting ethical, visionary and values-based human development.

Desmond Tutu is the author of nine collections of sermons and writings, including No Future without Forgiveness (London: Rider, 2000) and God Has a Dream: A Vision of Hope for Our Time (London: Rider, 2005).

John Allen, Rabble Rouser for Peace (New York: Free Press, 2006).

Michael Jesse Battle, Reconciliation: The Ubuntu Theology of Desmond Tutu (Pilgrim Press, 1997)

'IF YOU THINK YOU'RE SO ENLIGHTENED, GO AND SPEND A WEEK WITH YOUR PARENTS!'
RAM DASS, USA

# 11 GRATITUDE

## WHAT IS GRATITUDE?

Gratitude celebrates our connections with other beings and our capacity to offer mutual support. It is a form of openness and generosity that strengthens relationships and heals tension, resentment and anger. Gratitude calls us to strip away unnecessary complexities, and to be simple and natural with each other. It brings peace and harmony.

To receive gratitude from others is to strengthen our confidence that we have a positive role to play in the world. It makes us feel recognised, encouraged and inspired. When we are able to offer gratitude sincerely to someone else, notice how it brings a pleasant taste in the mouth, a warm feeling in the heart and a surge of energy. Appreciation feels good.

Gratitude is grounded in the wisdom which accepts that we are neither independent nor self-sufficient, but part of an extraordinary continuum of events and beings on this planet. It encourages us to welcome reality, rather than to fight it – both what seems good, and what seems bad. Learning to appreciate every single thing that happens as a potential source of insight and growth is one of the key ingredients for a happy life.

## WHY RAM DASS?

Ram Dass, formerly the American psychology professor Richard Alpert, was one of the 'high generation' hippies who experimented with narcotic substances in their search for truth. Gratitude did not necessarily fit well with their free thinking approach. They were rebels, many of whom kicked the dust of home from their shoes and disappeared for years on end to India. However Ram Dass went on to set up the Hanuman Foundation, to embody and celebrate the love and service that he had experienced there.

Ram Dass has described his life as being a succession of 'advance parties' – for the psychedelic movement (in the Sixties), for Westerners who were opening up to Eastern spirituality (in the Seventies), for a contemporary exploration of how everyday life can become spiritual practice (in the Eighties) and as a teacher on ageing and illness (in the Nineties). He has treated each one as a learning

'GRATITUDE IS NOT ONLY THE
GREATEST OF VIRTUES, BUT THE
PARENT OF ALL OTHERS' MARCUS
TULLIUS CICERO, ANCIENT ROME

experience, and as a result everything he has written and taught has been infused with thankfulness.

Ram Dass' early relationship with his parents was not easy, but as they grew older he consciously sought to repay their kindness to him. In *Still Here*, his book on ageing, change and dying, he describes the experience of becoming a carer for his father. At first it felt like a restriction and an intrusion on his life, but gradually he came to see it as a gift that shook him out of an egocentric attachment to external freedom.

Ram Dass has called for the 'heart to heart resuscitation of society.' He believes passionately that both personal and social transformation start with everyday attitudes such as gratitude and concern for others. He sees his work on himself as a gift to others, and a means to stem the cycle of pain and suffering in the world. He began his life seeking freedom through independence, but is ending it with the realisation that this is a contradiction: freedom can only be achieved through dependence on others.

## HOW DOES GRATITUDE LEAD TO HAPPINESS?

What happens when we express our gratitude to someone with a sincere 'thank you', a card or gift, a smile or a hug? For as long as the moment lasts, our eyes are soft, our bodies relaxed and our minds at peace. Something shifts inside and barriers drop away. When we can be genuinely grateful to each other, there is a special feeling in the air. Perhaps it is because we are admitting the reality that we can't do everything on our own.

'THE DEBT OF GRATITUDE THAT WE OWE OUR MOTHER AND FATHER GOES FORWARDS, NOT BACKWARDS. WHAT WE OWE OUR PARENTS IS THE BILL PRESENTED TO US BY OUR CHILDREN' NANCY FRIDAY, USA

To say 'thank you' is to reassure another person that they have the capacity to contribute to our well-being. It boosts confidence and self-respect, and can inspire them to continue being kind. To overlook what they have done for us is a form of rejection and sometimes of subtle humiliation. Do this and it gives the message that their contribution had no value.

The most powerful focus for our gratitude should logically be the adults who brought us into the world and looked after us in our early years. Without them we would never have learned to eat, dress, wash, or speak. Yet they are commonly the people we find it hardest to appreciate. It can be so difficult to drop our defences, overlook past difficulties, and admit how much we owe them. Our inability to do this can trigger years of pain.

**TRUE STORY:** The devastating tsunami that hit Asia and East Africa in December 2004 had a powerful effect on a Buddhist monk called the Venerable Thich Nguyen Thao. He decided to sell one of the meditation centres that he runs in Vancouver, Canada and donate the proceeds to the tsunami relief fund set up by the Canadian Red Cross. The donation was worth around half a million dollars. Venerable Nguyen described it as an expression of gratitude to the people of Indonesia, Thailand and Malaysia who had provided refuge to Vietnamese refugees such as himself. When the initial shock had worn off, his congregation commented that it was the best lesson they had ever received from their teacher. 'We can have a temple of compassion instead.'

We can see the power of gratitude in family life through the hurt that occurs when it is absent. Unfortunately this often manifests as judgement and criticism, or involves guilt and emotional manipulation. 'You should be grateful for this,' or 'You don't appreciate what I have done for you!' What are the inner knots that need to be undone?

**'A PERSON HOWEVER LEARNED AND QUALIFIED IN HIS LIFE'S WORK IN WHOM GRATITUDE IS ABSENT, IS DEVOID OF THAT BEAUTY OF CHARACTER WHICH MAKES PERSONALITY FRAGRANT'**
HAZRAT INAYAT KHAN, INDIA

Parents are not the only challenge. It can be equally difficult to show gratitude to the other people we are close to – our partners, our children and our oldest friends. Even if we have learned to give flowers or chocolate, or to organise parties and treats for special occasions, we may not be so good at acknowledging the small daily gestures of support and consideration.

Expressing appreciation depends more on our own mood and attitude rather than on what has been done for us. It seems to come more easily when we are feeling happy and confident. When we are defensive or preoccupied then we may not even notice what someone else is doing to support us. The other person can be left wondering if they did something wrong.

Gratitude has no meaning unless it is sincere. It is unfortunate that, every day, the phrase 'thank you' is cheapened and abused. Too often we say and write it without thinking. Our mouths or our keyboards move, but our eyes don't light up and our hearts fail to connect. 'Thank you' can even be said with sarcasm and anger. What can be done to turn this situation around?

Everyone loses out if we can't drop the ignorance or misconceptions that get in the way of gratitude. Years later we may realize the kindness of another and experience a piercing sense of loss at the fact that we never conveyed how much they and their efforts meant to us. When someone dies before we can express our gratitude, then death really calls us to account.

**'AS WE EXPRESS OUR GRATITUDE, WE MUST NEVER FORGET THAT THE HIGHEST APPRECIATION IS NOT TO UTTER WORDS, BUT TO LIVE BY THEM'** JOHN F KENNEDY, USA

Immense inner and outer benefits flow from honestly and humbly expressing gratitude to our parents and the many others who play a part in our lives – our teachers, brothers and sisters, relatives, coaches and mentors – everyone who helped us to be the person we are now. Can we find the courage and humility to seek them out and set the record straight? Even if the gifts they gave or the lessons they taught us were hard to swallow?

However difficult the past has been, it may be surprising to find out how much pleasure our appreciation will bring. One quick phone call or text message may instantly help someone to feel better about themselves. Caught up in our own thoughts, we assume they know how much they matter to us. But perhaps they don't. Appreciation sets the record straight and offers completion.

All too often, it takes a major crisis to pull us out of our self-sufficient isolation and trigger an expression of gratitude. It may feel daunting or impossible to re-enter old areas of our lives, with all their complexity and unresolved issues. There may be feelings of pain, guilt and regret. But it need not be as difficult as it seems and the sense of resolution can be extraordinary. Whether we like it or not, expressing and receiving gratitude is a basic human need.

**CHALLENGE:**  What is going well in your life? Can you identify six people who have contributed to this situation, either directly or indirectly? Have you expressed your appreciation? Some of them may be hard to thank. Is there a skilful way to do it?

## REFLECTION

- Find a quiet space where you can relax. Sit comfortably. To help you settle, focus your awareness on your breathing. Let go of any thoughts, images or feelings that arise. Whenever you become distracted, bring your awareness gently back to the sensation of the breath going in and out. Spend a few minutes enjoying the experience of coming to rest.

- Start by being grateful for all the good things that you experience in your life. Begin with physical things such as your home or possessions or surroundings. Recall that many people don't have these things, and that you may not always have them. Rejoice in your good fortune.

- Take the time to appreciate some less tangible things, such as your relationships, health, freedom and knowledge. Experience a sense of thankfulness and appreciation for each of the good things in your life.

- Turn your mind to the many people who have been kind to you in the past. Recall the relatives and friends who were supportive or kind to you when you were young. Remember the teachers who showed you how to read and write, or who inspired you to learn. Focus on as many specific incidents of kindness as you can.

- Spend some time imagining the kindnesses received from your parents. Begin in the womb, where your mother held you and fed you in her body. Think of how she nursed you as a baby, how she got up in the middle of the night to feed and comfort you. How she wiped you clean and made sure you were clothed. Silently express your gratitude to her.

- Recall how, as a small child, you were completely dependent on the kindness of an adult. You were fed, washed and put to bed. You were taught to walk and taken to school. To whatever extent you can, expand these feelings of gratitude and affection.

- See how all the love and kindness you have received in your life depended on similar love and kindness in previous generations. Imagine this kindness reaching back over millennia. Can you develop a wish to repay and pass on this vast kindness?

- Close with the wish 'May all beings be happy!'

## RESOURCES

www.ramdass.org includes live streaming from Ram Dass's centre on Maui, Hawaii, multimedia reference materials and an interactive online community.

The Hanuman Foundation, www.hanumanfoundation.com, was founded on the life principles of Ram Dass's Indian teacher Neem Karoli Baba, who taught to 'Love and feed people,' and to 'Love and serve everyone.'

Ram Dass' many books include: Be Here Now (New York: Crown Publishing Group, 1971), How Can I Help? Stories and Reflections on Service written with Paul Gorman (Alfred A Knopf, 2002) and Still Here: Embracing Ageing, Changing and Dying (New York: Riverhead Books, 2001).

'Fierce Grace', directed by Mickey Lemle, 2002 (Region 1 DVD/Video released by Zeitgeist Films, 2003).

**'TO LIVE THE FULL LIFE, ONE MUST HAVE THE COURAGE TO BEAR
RESPONSIBILITY FOR THE NEEDS OF OTHERS'**
AUNG SAN SUU KYI, BURMA

# 12 LOYALTY

## WHAT IS LOYALTY?

When life is going well, it's easy to forget that change happens in an instant. It is the nature of the universe. In an uncertain world, a sense of loyalty and mutual responsibility is often the glue that holds families and friendships together. It can be the lifeline that helps us to feel safe and supported and enables us to function well.

We all want to be accepted for who we are. Not for what we can buy, what we look like or who we know. When we cannot rely on the loyalty of each other, there is anxiety and insecurity, loneliness and heartbreak.

It is logical to feel loyalty towards the people we feel close to, especially if we want them to be loyal to us. But can this feeling of closeness go further? Is it possible to extend the same warmth and support to people outside our inner circle? What can be done to develop an attitude of loyalty and solidarity towards the wider community and, ultimately, towards the entire planet? Some great people, such as the role models in this book, seem able to do this. What would the world be like if we could each extend our sense of loyalty in this way?

## WHY AUNG SAN SUU KYI?

Aung San Suu Kyi inherited her profound sense of loyalty and duty towards the Burmese people from her father, Aung Sang, who helped achieve independence for Burma in the early twentieth century. She describes him as 'a man who put the interests of the country before his own needs, who remained poor and unassuming at the height of his power, who accepted the responsibilities of leadership without hankering after the privileges.'

In 1971, in the months that led up to her marriage, Suu Kyi wrote a poignant letter to her English fiancé, Michael Aris. 'I only ask one thing, that should my people need me, you would help me to do my duty by them.' It was an extremely painful dilemma. 'Sometimes I am beset by fears that circumstances and national considerations might tear us apart just when we are so happy in each other that separation would be a torment.'

In the late 1980s, she had to choose between these two conflicting loyalties. Suu Kyi became the leader of the Burmese National League for Democracy and was imprisoned by the military regime. By the end of 2006 she had spent over 10 of the previous 17 years under house arrest in the capital city of Rangoon. Her main contact with the outside world has been a shortwave radio and a monthly visit from her doctor. She has not seen her children grow up, and could not be with her husband when he died of cancer. No wonder she proposes: 'The quintessential revolution is that of the spirit.'

**'WE MUST LOVE FRIENDS FOR THEIR SAKE RATHER THAN FOR OUR OWN' CHARLOTTE BRONTE, UK**

Suu Kyi's strength grows out of the conviction that taking responsibility for the happiness and well-being of others will bring happiness for herself. She believes: 'We must all understand that there is great merit in sacrificing for others and that by so doing we live the full life.'

## HOW DOES LOYALTY LEAD TO HAPPINESS?

What makes us care enough to speak up or stand up for someone else, no matter what? To make a public gesture, and experience whatever personal inconvenience, discomfort or challenges this brings? The call to action comes from something in our guts. If we don't respond in some way, we die a little. Our spirit fades.

The person who chooses to be loyal is asking 'What can I do for you? How can I make your life easier or more comfortable?' It is a fundamental shift of focus. When we can do this with one person, we can do it with others. It doesn't happen simply because we perceive our interests to be bound up with those of the people whom we love. We have an instinct that happiness begins when we can consider the welfare of others to be as important as our own.

**'IT'S THE FRIENDS YOU CAN CALL UP AT 4 AM THAT MATTER' MARLENE DIETRICH, GERMANY**

Taking responsibility for each other is the key to survival in both the human and the animal realms. It is a sign of growth and maturity when the adult can demonstrate concern for the well-being of others. Without it, there is no basis for the rule of law, for community, for family and for child-raising. Perhaps this is why everyone respects people who are loyal. It is one of the most common themes in films, books, newspapers and on TV.

The loyal friend will voice the awkward truth that we struggle to hear. They will listen to us when we are anxious or depressed, and comfort us when things go wrong. They will do their best to be patient and forgiving. If we know that a friend

**TRUE STORY:** Sandra Aguebor is an energetic mother of two from Lagos, Nigeria, who is known as the Lady Mechanic. She started out by stopping to help other women whose cars had broken down on chaotic, crime-ridden Lagos streets and giving them a quick lesson in basic car maintenance while she changed tyres or got their cars started. In 2000 she raised the money to start the Lady Mechanic Initiative, which now provides training for over 70 underprivileged or vulnerable young women. As well as creating employment and business opportunities in an area previously regarded as 'men-only', Aguebor teaches basic book keeping skills, provides subsidised health insurance and gives out toolkits on graduation. She also revels in her position as a women's role model. 'I have broken the yoke of shame, of fear of the unknown – you know, women fear a lot.'

See the article by Sarah Simpson, which first appeared in **The Christian Science Monitor,** www.csmonitor.com

or colleague will be loyal to us no matter what happens, then we will explore how to live with greater reassurance and can take more risks. When our back is covered, it becomes far easier to face outwards with confidence and a sense of freedom.

Loyalty helps us to worry less about every little thing we say or do. When the fundamentals are taken care of, and a deep level of trust exists, then loving action flows more easily and imaginatively. We can relate to one another in a more open, relaxed and transparent way.

We have a special relationship with the friends who embrace us just as we are, through all the different phases of our lives and regardless of how we behave. Rough and smooth, rebellious and conservative, rational and irrational. They may not agree with all our principles and values, or the choices that we make. We may not see them for years, but we know we can still count on them.

People whose lives are full of hardship and adversity, such as refugee communities, often have the strongest appreciation for the value of loyalty and the difference it can make. It can mean they are better at surviving, and even at being happy, than people whose lives are smoother and easier.

**'THOU SHALT NOT BE A VICTIM. THOU SHALT NOT BE A PERPETRATOR. ABOVE ALL, THOU SHALT NOT BE A BYSTANDER'** HOLOCAUST MUSEUM, NEW YORK

In prosperous countries, people become homeless when their last bit of support disappears. There is a pivotal moment when they are no longer welcome on someone's floor or sofa. When they pick up whatever possessions they can fit into a bag, and slip out of the door to go and sleep on the street. After this, life only turns around when a homeless person finds a friend or worker who can stand up for their needs and support them – someone who demonstrates loyalty to them as human beings, and a sense of responsibility for their welfare.

Our support for charitable activity highlights how much value we place on loyalty, both in our own lives and as a society. We also need to ask ourselves how often we visit our elderly relatives, how closely we stay in touch with old friends (even if they don't fit in with our current crowd) and how often we avoid a friend because they're going through a difficult patch and aren't such good company at the moment.

Loyalty and responsibility can feel like a heavy burden that threatens to steal our joy. Blind loyalty can lead us astray and undermine our judgement. But expressing loyalty also brings energy and satisfaction – that we have something to offer, that we can choose to act for the good of others and, that we are not alone.

**CHALLENGE:** Are you close to someone who is having a difficult time at the moment? Take a few quiet moments to consider their situation and their needs. Is there something practical you can do to support them? Are you willing to do it? If not, is something holding you back?

## REFLECTION

- Find a quiet space where you can relax. Sit comfortably. To help you settle, focus your awareness on your breathing. Let go of any thoughts, images or feelings that arise. Whenever you become distracted, bring your awareness gently back to the sensation of the breath going in and out. Spend a few minutes enjoying the experience of coming to rest.

- If you have a garden, imagine yourself looking at it now. If you don't have one, then imagine that you do. Your garden contains flower and plants, perhaps even vegetables and fruit trees. Some parts of your garden are spectacular – these are the areas you have given time and attention to. What do they look like? Some parts of your garden are straggly and neglected. What do they look like?

- Consider the idea: Whatever we pay attention to will grow; whatever we neglect will decline. Is this true for your garden?

- Your garden is a metaphor for your relationships. Reflect on those you have neglected by not meeting up for a chat, phoning, emailing or simply not paying attention. Why have you been neglecting them? Without resorting to guilt or blame, calmly ask yourself, 'Have I been a loyal friend to these people?'

- In comparison, reflect on the relationships that receive your time and attention. These are the flourishing and well-tended areas of your garden. What causes you to be affectionate and loyal to some people and not to others? How do you demonstrate your loyalty?

- Ask yourself, 'What does loyalty mean for me?'

- What would it take to pay equal attention to the whole of your garden? How would it look if every corner was alive with colour and foliage? How would you feel if every tree, plant and blade of grass was green and flourishing? How much effort would this require? Are you willing to dedicate the necessary time and energy? Watch your emotions around this question and calmly acknowledge them – there may be guilt, shame, a sense of heaviness.

- What attention are you willing to give your garden at this moment?

- Close with the wish 'May all beings be happy!'

## RESOURCES

There are more than 20 organisations worldwide dedicated to the campaign for human rights and democracy in Burma. See www.burmacampaign.org.uk for more information.

Freedom from Fear: And Other Writings (London: Penguin, 1995) is a collection of articles by Aung San Suu Kyi with other material, including forewords by Desmond Tutu and Vaclav Havel.

Aung San Suu Kyi, Letters from Burma (London: Penguin, 1997) and The Voice of Hope (London: Penguin, 2002).

Barbara Victor, The Lady: Aung San Suu Kyi: Nobel Laureate and Burma's Prisoner (London: Faber and Faber, 2002).

# HOW WE
# FIND
# MEANING

# If everything is changing, anything is possible

Change is all around us. It is a law of nature. As the world revolves, day turns to night, seasons come and go, food grows and decays, machines are invented and become obsolete, and new clothes once the height of fashion become faded and worn. Across the millennia, even mountains and continents are on the move.

Living beings are also caught up in a constant process of change. The atoms that make up our bodies are in flux. We are born, we grow up, we reach adulthood, and then we get old and die. In every moment, our thoughts and emotions are shifting, often faster than we can realise.

Everything that is produced and created has a lifecycle that is subject to change and decay. Ignoring this basic truth traps us in illusion – clinging to the idea that things endure and remain stable, despite all the evidence to the contrary. We forget that a treasured cup will break, a loving relationship may falter, a flower will wilt, or that our family, friends and pets will grow old. When we fail to appreciate this, our lack of understanding can cause incredible discomfort and pain in our lives.

Even if we know deep down that things will change, we try to ignore the fact. Change can be scary. What will the future hold? Will it be better or worse, easier or harder, more sad or more happy? Yet a life without change would be unthinkable, devoid of opportunity and hope. We would be stuck just as we are, without the opportunity to grow or develop. If we can make wise decisions about how to spend our time and energy, change is something to be welcomed and embraced. There is infinite potential in every moment - and it is up to you whether you choose to grasp it.

Your search for meaning will depend on your ability and willingness to explore new and unfamiliar territory. This is why it is often called a 'path'. It is a challenge to venture deep into yourself, to explore your inner strength and longings, and find out how to use them to create a happy and fulfilling life. The process may be tough, demanding and exhausting, but also thrilling, liberating and profound. Who are you? What are you doing here? How can you make the best of the years you spend on this earth?

The role models in this section are people who went on this personal journey, and who found meaning through abandoning a narrow and self-centred view of themselves and the world. They demonstrate how developing aspirations, principles, service and courage can help you to find happiness for yourself and others.

**'WE ARE THE GENERATION WE HAVE BEEN WAITING FOR'**
CRAIG KIELBURGER, CANADA

# 13 ASPIRATION

## WHAT IS ASPIRATION?

Aspiration is the profound longing for purpose and fulfilment, joy and happiness, which lies deep – and sometimes buried – in our hearts, and in the heart of every living being. It is the voice inside that urges us to use our life well and to make the best of whatever gifts and passions we possess. The way we choose to respond to that voice will determine all the other choices we make in our lives.

Simply to pick up this book is to aspire. Aspiration is the fuel of change. It feeds on our hope that life could be better or more meaningful, and our willingness to do something differently to make this happen. It is a call to action.

**'I'VE OFTEN SAID, THE ONLY THING STANDING BETWEEN ME AND GREATNESS IS ME'**
WOODY ALLEN, USA

Everyone aspires to be happy, and it is a natural human quality to include others in this aspiration. We want our family and friends to be prosperous and content. We want homeless people to find shelter, hungry people to have food, sick people to have medicine. We want the world to be at peace.

The happiest and most contented people are usually those who have found a way to put their aspirations for self and others into practice, and have thereby played an active part in creating a better world. This is the common characteristic of all the role models in this book. Their life stories may seem daunting and out of reach. In hindsight they are towering figures. Yet everything they did consisted of small choices and steps, many of which are possible for anyone.

What can we do to turn our own aspirations into reality? How can we taste and realise our unique potential as human beings?

## WHY CRAIG KIELBURGER?

Craig Kielburger was 12 years old when he saw a newspaper headline about a Pakistani boy, Iqbal Masih, who had been murdered for speaking out about the working conditions he had endured in the carpet-making industry. From that moment, Craig's life began to change. He photocopied the article, went down to the local library to research statistics on child labour, and invited some of his classmates round for 'pop and pizza' to discuss what they could do to improve the lives of children on the other side of the world.

Twelve years later, Craig's organisation Free the Children has inspired more than a million young people to get involved in humanitarian activities. It builds schools, provides healthcare, improves sanitation and supports small business development in more than 45 countries. Its mission is to free children everywhere from abuse or exploitation, and from the idea that they are not old enough, smart enough or capable enough to change the world. Free the Children is also funded, driven and staffed by children and youth.

**'A TREE THAT CAN FILL THE SPAN OF A MAN'S ARMS GROWS FROM A DOWNY TIP; A TERRACE NINE STOREYS HIGH RISES FROM HODFULS OF EARTH; A JOURNEY OF A THOUSAND MILES STARTS FROM BENEATH ONE'S FEET'**
LAO TZU, CHINA

In parallel with their humanitarian work, Craig and his brother Marc campaign about the importance of helping young people to realise their aspirations. In 1999 they established Leaders Today, an organization that provides leadership training to more than 350,000 young people each year. They run a website (www.globalvoices.org) that encourages young people to report on and discuss global issues. Their most recent book, *From Me to We*, proposes that every young person has an issue that hits them in the heart – and that the challenge is to act on it. 'Find your gift. Find your passion. Put them together and you will change the world. It only takes one small act to make a difference.'

## HOW DOES ASPIRATION LEAD TO HAPPINESS?

There is nothing wrong with eating, sleeping, going to work, shopping, seeing movies or making love. But will you find satisfaction if your entire life is taken up with the pursuit of pleasure and personal comfort? It can become like salty water that never quenches your thirst, and the result may be nothing more than quiet desperation. The happiest human beings seem to be those who have created some meaning to their existence beyond simply taking care of themselves.

Even if we are scared, aspiration makes our blood sing and our eyes shine. These are the moments when we sense that anything is possible – that human beings can create great beauty, resolve intractable problems, show vast compassion and develop enduring wisdom.

How often do you reflect on what really fires you up? Can you give a day, an hour or even five minutes to honestly ask this question? Where is the resistance?

**TRUE STORY:** When mother-of-two Jane Tomlinson was diagnosed with breast cancer in 1990, she started a three-year radiography course at hospitals in her native Yorkshire, UK – not as a patient, but as a trainee radiographer. It proved to be only the start of an extraordinarily spirited response to her illness. When the cancer returned, her son was only three and she decided she wanted to achieve something that he could be proud of. Jane undertook an extraordinary series of sporting challenges, which included cycle rides across Europe and the USA, the world's first marathon run on chemotherapy, the 2004 Ironman triathlon and a 4,200-mile cycle ride from San Francisco to New York. In the process she raised over £1.75 million for respite care, nursing and cancer research. Jane died in September 2007, nearly seven years after being given only six months to live. The motto of the Jane Appeal is 'Death doesn't arrive with the prognosis'.

Is it the risk of admitting that you may not be satisfied? Does part of you long for change while another part is anxious and afraid? Are you willing to acknowledge your power and potential to shape your life in the way that you long for?

King Songtsen Gampo proposed that there are three interlocking components that will help us to explore and channel our aspirations. Firstly, a teacher or teachers to inspire and guide us; secondly a set of teachings to listen and reflect on, and thirdly a set of companions who are moving in the same direction as ourselves. When all three are in place, we will have a stable foundation for finding meaning in life.

There are teachers all around us - what does it take to find one who can kindle a fire in our heart, while also being reliable and honest? What other qualities do you look for in a teacher? This is such an important matter that it is wise to check up very carefully, perhaps even over a period of years. Are you seeking a teacher within a religious tradition, or

> **'VISION IS NOT ENOUGH; IT MUST BE COMBINED WITH VENTURE.'**
> VACLAV HAVEL, CZECH REPUBLIC

elsewhere? Some people will travel long distances, while for others, it will happen on their own doorstep, perhaps in a quiet moment when preconceptions have dropped away.

Teachings can take manifold forms. There is now unparalleled access to the great religious, philosophical and wisdom traditions of the world, not only through talks and books but on the internet and in the media. Look out for poetry that touches your heart, music that moves us you, the novel that brings a flash of insight, or the film that stays with you for days afterwards. To be inspired is like breathing different air.

If we really want to shift our focus and direction, the third pillar of support will be like-minded friends or companions. When we aspire to achieve a goal or make a change in our lives, we set out on a journey. Having companions to share advice and lift our spirits can make all the difference. If we take on a demanding job, is there someone we can turn to when things are tough? If we choose to support a good cause, is there a group who share our concerns? If we follow a spiritual path, is there a community of people who will encourage us to stay on track?

Aspiration raises the stakes. When it is not followed through, it can turn sour. The heart grieves for what has been tasted but lost. Yet when aspiration leads us into action, we feel a transformation – and usually we look different too. Bad news and disappointments are faced with more equanimity. We have a greater urgency to ease the suffering of others. We feel more at peace. Even in the darkest moments there is hope.

**CHALLENGE:** Do you ever dream of how to make the world a better place? What would you like to see happen that is so big and inspiring that it would take more than one lifetime to accomplish? Are you willing to start it now? What would be the first small step?

## REFLECTION

- Find a quiet space where you can relax. Sit comfortably. To help you settle, focus your awareness on your breathing. Let go of any thoughts, images or feelings that arise. Whenever you become distracted, bring your awareness gently back to the sensation of the breath going in and out. Spend a few minutes enjoying the experience of coming to rest.

- Bring your awareness to the body. What is it made of? Think about the different parts like skin, blood, bones and organs, which in turn are made of cells, which in turn are made of atoms, subatomic particles and so forth. Reflect on how all these cells are moving, changing, dividing and dying. Try to feel the energy and movement within your body.

- Now take this awareness outside of yourself. Reflect on how the furniture, glass, floor and everything around you is also made up of tiny particles, which are constantly changing from one millisecond to the next. Open your senses to the world: listen to its dynamic energy and observe its constant process of transformation.

- Widen your awareness to include the billions of people and animals on this planet whose bodies are also moving and changing. Observe the concrete cities, countryside, mountains and seas; the sun, moon, stars and clouds. Can you find anything that is static?

- Next, imagine pushing a 'Stop!' button. Suddenly the world becomes still as a statue. Everything comes to a halt. What would this be like?

- Bring your awareness back to yourself. You too have come to a standstill. What would this be like? What effect would it have on your mind, your body, your behaviour? How could you dream, learn or grow? How could you fulfil your dreams and aspirations?

- Release the stop button. Everything starts moving again and you have regained your freedon. Ponder the idea: if everything is changing, anything is possible.

- Close with the wish 'May all beings be happy.'

## RESOURCES

www.freethechildren.com features resources such as Take Action! A Guide to Active Citizenship; Take More Action and 7 Steps to Social Involvement.

www.metowe.org is an online community for anyone inspired by the recent book by Crail Kielburger and Marc Kielburger, Me to We: Finding Meaning in a Material World (New York: Fireside, 2006).

www.leaderstoday.com is the website of a worldwide youth leadership organisation set up by Craig and Marc Kielburger.

Craig Kielburger and Kevin Major, Free the Children: A Young Man Fights Against Child Labor and Proves That Children Can Change The World (New York: Harper Perennial, 1999).

'It Takes a Child: Craig Kielburger's Story – A Journey into Child Labour', directed by Judy Jackson, 1998 (DVD/Video distributed by Bullfrog Films) won the UNESCO Gold Award at The New York Festival.

**'WE CANNOT ABDICATE OUR CONSCIENCE TO AN ORGANIZATION, NOR TO A GOVERNMENT'**
ALBERT SCHWEITZER, GERMANY/FRANCE

# 14 PRINCIPLES

## WHAT ARE PRINCIPLES?

If we were each given a blank sheet of paper, how many of us would be able to list the principles that guide our lives? Day-to-day living makes so many demands that sometimes it feels more than enough just to react as best we can to whatever happens, hoping it will all turn out OK.

Yet most of us have plenty of principles, even if we are not aware of them. What is it that angers us or gets the fire churning in our gut? Getting upset is often the sign that a principle we hold strongly has been breached. It touches on something that says 'No!' We may be surprised by the passion and strength that is alive in us.

Principles give us strength. They provide the foundations from which we get the power and energy to make a stand about the things that matter to us. They keep our aspirations on track. Like the spokes of a bicycle wheel, they give stability and help us move forward in a purposeful way. What can we each do to be true to our principles, and to use them skilfully to build a happy life?

## WHY ALBERT SCHWEITZER?

During his twenties, Albert Schweitzer was a prosperous and successful Christian pastor, musician and academic in Strasbourg, Germany. What almost no-one knew was that he had made a personal vow to change his life at the age of thirty. Highly critical of the contemporary Church, he wanted not simply to talk about Jesus' life of compassionate service, but to put it into practice. To the surprise and dismay of family and friends, Schweitzer re-trained as a medical doctor and set off to found a hospital at Lambaréné in French Equatorial Africa.

The principle of 'Reverence for Life' which Schweitzer developed during his years in Africa was rooted in what he later described as the most powerful experience of his youth. When out with a friend shooting at some birds with a catapult, Schweitzer realised that he did not want to kill. From that day onwards he tried always to follow his own principles, regardless of what anyone thought or said about him. 'Never for a moment do we lay aside our mistrust of the ideals established by society, and of the convictions which are kept by it in circulation.'

Later in life, the left-handed Schweitzer taught himself to write with his right hand rather than disturb the cat which habitually slept on his left arm. It is a small but poignant example of his principle 'a man's life is the same as his thought.'

**'AN UNEASY CONSCIENCE IS A HAIR IN THE MOUTH'**
MARK TWAIN, USA

For Schweitzer, our inner moral being perishes if we become too tired to share the life, experiences and sufferings of the creatures around us. 'Woe to us if our sensitivity grows numb. It destroys our conscience in the broadest sense of the word: the consciousness of how we should act dies.'

Schweitzer had an outstanding intellect and was a free thinker for whom nothing was off limits. However he believed that unless our values are rooted in both the rational and the mystical/emotional aspects of our being, then they will lack vitality. In line with this, he never saw 'Reverence for Life' as a set of rules, but rather as a basic principle to guide the difficult decisions that each individual is called to make.

## HOW DO PRINCIPLES LEAD TO HAPPINESS?

The function of principles is to be our inner compass, a touchstone for who we are and what we want to do with our lives. They make us unique. It is a risky business to ignore them. We may find we give away our peace of mind.

Principles prevent us from being a victim of circumstance. They act as a bridge between the quiet times when we listen to what we feel inside, and the busy times when there is no time to think before we speak or act. Discipline and habit can help us stay on track. Following what we value is a relief.

To reflect on our principles is to hold a conversation with ourselves. What is it that matters most to us? What kind of principles do we want to be known for – at work, among our friends and family, or even after our death? Do we want to be

**'THIS ABOVE ALL: TO THINE OWN SELF BE TRUE, AND IT MUST FOLLOW, AS THE NIGHT THE DAY, THOU CANST NOT THEN BE FALSE TO ANY MAN'**
WILLIAM SHAKESPEARE, UK

remembered as someone who always stood up for what they felt was right, who played fair, who told the truth and treated people well? Or as someone who was 'unprincipled'?

Our values and principles come alive at the edge, in the difficult moments, and when we feel under threat. They mark the point when we stand up for ourselves and do something different, when we do not just melt into the crowd and go along with an action that does

**TRUE STORY:**

A famous experiment was conducted at Princeton University in 1973, in which a group of theology students was asked to walk across campus to deliver a sermon on the topic of the Good Samaritan. As part of the research, some of the students were told that they were late and needed to hurry. Along the route, the researchers Darley and Batson had placed an actor, who was lying on the ground in pain and in need of help. In their haste to give a sermon on compassion, 90% of the 'late' students from Princeton Theology Seminary completely ignored the needs of the suffering person. Some of them literally stepped over him.

not feel right. To stick by our principles in the face of temptation, shows that we are capable of taking responsibility for our lives.

Every day we create the causes and conditions for the future. If our goal is the happiness of self and others, we need to pay careful attention. The millions of tiny decisions we make, each multiply into millions more. What are the principles that will guide us skilfully through these endless possibilities?

Many people will try to influence our principles, especially when we are young. It is a common dimension of family life, school and entertainment. At what point does this become counter-productive? 'I want to make up my own mind!' Somehow we know that principles need to be owned, not borrowed. The very act of developing them is a process of discovering what has meaning for us. It is the way we find our voice.

**'THE WHOLE PROBLEM WITH THE WORLD IS THAT FOOLS AND FANATICS ARE ALWAYS SO CERTAIN OF THEMSELVES, BUT WISER PEOPLE SO FULL OF DOUBTS'**
BERTRAND RUSSELL, UK

Principles help us make friends and work together for good causes. They are a message, a badge of identity, which inspires confidence about who we are, how we operate and what we represent. If we know someone will never tell a lie, then we also know we will never be deceived by them. If we know they will never resort to physical force, then we are not at risk of violence. Our principles can make us a refuge for everyone around us.

It is a mistake to see principles as dull and predictable. The opposite is often the case. It can be exciting to be around people with strong principles. They are often the dynamic free-thinkers. They have energy and confidence, and make bold choices about how they spend their time. Like the role models in this book, they can draw us like a magnet.

Unfortunately, it can also be contagious to spend time with people whose principles are less developed. 'It's fine to make personal calls from work...don't worry, everyone makes fun of him...it doesn't matter if you help yourself to more.' If we're not clear about where we stand, it is tempting to go with the crowd. Yet it is niggling and uncomfortable to behave in a way that does not feel right. It sits uneasily, and whispers to us in the middle of the night. Are we willing to admit that we have let ourselves down and, if so, what does this actually mean?

If we want to use our principles as a benchmark or standard against which we check ourselves, then humility and humour are essential. Do we dare to review the day's activities before we go to sleep? Can we be kind and patient with ourselves when we slip up? Our principles offer a reminder that we are all 'works in progress.'

**CHALLENGE:**  What are the issues that you are passionate about? Why do they fire you up? What do they tell you about yourself? Take a few minutes to identify your own personal guidelines on how to think and behave. Talk them over with a friend. Do you manage to live up to them? If not, what can you do about it?

## REFLECTION

- Find a quiet space where you can relax. Sit comfortably. To help you settle, focus your awareness on your breathing. Let go of any thoughts, images or feelings that arise. Whenever you become distracted, bring your awareness gently back to the sensation of the breath going in and out. Spend a few minutes enjoying the experience of coming to rest.

- Pose yourself the question 'What are my principles?' Let the question gradually descend within you, like a leaf dropping into a deep well. Repeat this a few times.

- Recall a time when you felt calm and solid, like a mountain with foundations stretching far down into the earth. Focus all your attention on the sensation of being grounded and centred. What was going on at that time? What were you thinking? What were you doing? Be as precise as you can.

- Now recall a time when you felt wobbly and unsure of yourself or when you were unfocused and confused. What was going on at that time? What were you thinking? What were you doing? Be as precise as you can.

● Replay each of these situations in your mind. How do the memories manifest in your body? Can you observe any particular sensations in your belly, heart, or throat? Gently probe what these sensations are.

● Ask yourself 'What are the values and principles that ground me – that create the sense of being like a mountain?' Identify whatever words, images or ideas come into your mind. If you do not know where to start, try using a 'ready-made' list of principles such as the ten commandments.

● As you examine each value and principle, continue to watch the sensations that arise in your body and notice where there is tension or softness. Can you use these sensations to identify which values and principles are the most alive in you? Do you know why this is so?

● Rest in the strength of whichever values and principles have the most meaning for you.

● Close with the wish 'May all beings be happy!'

## RESOURCES

www.albertschweitzer.info provides a range of resources including a set of short stories from Schweitzer's life.

James Brabazon, Albert Schweitzer: Essential Writings. (Maryknoll: Orbis Books, 2005).

Albert Schweitzer, Out of My Life and Thought. Trans. by Antje Bultmann. (Baltimore: Johns Hopkins University Press, 1998). Orig. published 1933.

Albert Schweitzer, Memoirs of Childhood and Youth. Trans. by Kurt Bergel and Alice R. Bergel (Syracuse: Syracuse University Press, 1997).

James Brabazon, Albert Schweitzer: A Biography. 2nd edn. (Syracuse: Syracuse University Press, 2000).

'Albert Schweitzer', restored and Uncut (film). Directed by Jerome Hill, 1957. (released on DVD/Video by Roan Archival Group in 2005). Won an Academy Award for Best Documentary in 1957.

'LIFE'S PERSISTENT AND MOST URGENT QUESTION IS:
WHAT ARE YOU DOING FOR OTHERS?'
MARTIN LUTHER KING JR, USA

# 15 SERVICE

## WHAT IS SERVICE?

Service is the outer expression of a wish to benefit others – to increase their happiness. At its best, it is an expression of caring, sharing, and delighting in each other. When it arises effortlessly and spontaneously, it is beautiful to watch. Service can also be experienced as a duty. Instead of being light and joyful, it feels heavy and burdensome. For most of us, learning how to serve – and to be served – is a lifetime's task.

In every moment there is an opportunity to make someone else's life a little bit easier or nicer. Every thought, word and action that flows from us in a loving way has the potential to create happiness. Are we willing to find within ourselves the sensitivity and intelligence, the clarity and conviction that this will take?

The rewards are huge. As we discover and deepen our wish for other people to be happy, we also find the key to our own happiness. Nobody gets left out of the equation. This is the golden rule of heart-felt service that underpins the great spiritual and wisdom traditions of the world. 'Do unto others as you would have them do to yourself.'

> 'IT IS ONE OF THE BEAUTIFUL COMPENSATIONS OF THIS LIFE THAT NO ONE CAN SINCERELY TRY TO HELP ANOTHER WITHOUT HELPING HIMSELF' RALPH WALDO EMERSON, USA

## WHY MARTIN LUTHER KING JR?

'An individual has not started living until he can rise above the narrow confines of his individualistic concerns to the broader concerns of all humanity.' Martin Luther King demonstrated this principle not only in his words but also in the way he dedicated his life to the struggle for justice and peace. 'As long as there is poverty in the world I can never be rich, even if I have a billion dollars... I can never be what I ought to be until you are what you ought to be. This is the way our world is made.'

King's views were grounded not only in his Christian faith but also in a vision of common humanity. 'All men are interdependent. Every nation is an heir of a vast treasure of ideas and labour to which both the living and the dead of all nations have contributed. Whether we realise it or not, each of us lives eternally "in the red".' His commitment to justice and equality was similarly down to earth. As King said in his 1963 'Strength to Love' speech, 'The good neighbour looks beyond the external accidents and discerns those inner qualities that make all men human and, therefore, brothers.'

**'EVEN A SMALL STAR SHINES IN THE DARKNESS'**
FINNISH PROVERB

King's argument rests on the realisation that to love and serve each other is a natural consequence of our shared humanity. It is the true sign of civilization and progress. Behind some of his most moving speeches, it is possible to sense his frustration at our inability to understand that 'We must learn to live together as brothers, or perish together as fools!'

Martin Luther King's tireless campaign for black dignity and equality was the external expression of his belief in love and service without limits. When he accepted the Nobel Peace Prize he described it as a commission to go out and work even harder for the things that he believed in.

**'HOW CAN I BE USEFUL, OF WHAT SERVICE CAN I BE? THERE IS SOMETHING INSIDE ME – WHAT CAN IT BE?'**
VINCENT VAN GOGH, FRANCE

Martin Luther King's 'Drum Major Speech' was delivered in Atlanta, Georgia in 1968, a few months before his assassination. It sums up his vision for how to lead a happy and meaningful life. 'If you want to be important – wonderful. If you want to be recognized – wonderful. If you want to be great – wonderful. But recognize that he who is greatest among you shall be your servant. That's a new definition of greatness.... By giving that definition of greatness it means that everybody can be great. Because everybody can serve...You only need a heart full of grace. A soul generated by love.'

## HOW DOES SERVICE LEAD TO HAPPINESS?

People who continually serve others, such as the role models in this book, act in this way because it brings them a sense of purpose and joy. They provide tangible evidence that working for the well-being of others can be a source of happiness. The more they give, the more energy they seem to have.

There are opportunities for listening and giving all around us, over cups of tea, at bedsides and on park benches. It doesn't mean we have to live in the slums, work on a hospital ward, or teach at a challenging school. In offering service we learn skills and make friends. We shift our attention away from our own anxieties and concerns. We strengthen and support the society in which we live. The Dalai Lama calls this being 'wisely selfish.'

**TRUE STORY:** Tim Lefens never saw himself as a 'kind' person – he was a successful and self-centred artist who loved surfing, women and motorbikes. But in the early 1990s, he agreed to show some slides of his work at a centre for the severely disabled. His book 'Flying Colors' describes how that day changed his life. He unexpectedly found his gaze held by a man in a wheelchair, whose body was agonisingly contorted but whose indestructible spirit shone out of his eyes. Lefens became obsessed with helping physically disabled people to express their inner spirit through painting. He has now developed a system by which they can direct a trained studio assistant to apply the paint, using a laser attached to a headband. The results have been extraordinary, selling in some of the most important galleries in New York City. Tim describes his work as 'not based on helping the less fortunate, but on bringing full, uncompromised creative power to people whose thoughts and feelings are simply trapped by their body's limitations.' The organization he set up is called Artistic Realization Technologies www.artrealization.org.

Is there anyone who doesn't feel good when they do something well for someone else? It's nice to see a smile or hear a 'thank you'. But what we are really seeking is the sense of satisfaction that arises in the heart. Even as children we are attracted to this pleasurable sensation. Why is it that serving others brings satisfaction and meaning, whereas serving ourselves frequently leads to disappointment? And if this is the case, what does it take to act accordingly?

The people who serve the most deeply and sincerely seem to be those who can expose themselves the most fully to another person's needs and problems. It can be painful and difficult to open up to the suffering of someone else. Our minds recoil, seeking a more pleasurable focus of attention. Yet if we can stay open and aware, we may find the answer for many of our own needs and dilemmas.

As meditators and hermits have shown across the centuries, it is possible to develop a profound level of empathy through using our powers of reasoning and imagination. The starting point is

'THIS IS THE TRUE JOY OF LIFE, THE BEING USED UP FOR A PURPOSE RECOGNISED BY YOURSELF AS A MIGHTY ONE; BEING A FORCE OF NATURE INSTEAD OF A FEVERISH, SELFISH, LITTLE CLOD OF AILMENTS AND GRIEVANCES, COMPLAINING THAT THE WORLD WILL NOT DEVOTE ITSELF TO MAKING YOU HAPPY. I AM OF THE OPINION THAT MY LIFE BELONGS TO THE COMMUNITY, AND AS LONG AS I LIVE, IT IS MY PRIVILEGE TO DO FOR IT WHATEVER I CAN. I WANT TO BE THOROUGHLY USED UP WHEN I DIE, FOR THE HARDER I WORK THE MORE I LIVE. LIFE IS NO 'BRIEF CANDLE' TO ME. IT IS A SORT OF SPLENDID TORCH WHICH I HAVE GOT HOLD OF FOR A MOMENT, AND I WANT TO MAKE IT BURN AS BRIGHTLY AS POSSIBLE BEFORE HANDING IT ON TO FUTURE GENERATIONS'
GEORGE BERNARD SHAW, UK

to deepen our awareness of how much we have in common with other living beings. Just as we want to avoid hunger, thirst, unkindness, cruelty or violence, so do they. Daily reflections of this kind help to generate and sustain a heartfelt desire for all our fellow beings to be happy, or at least to be free from suffering. As the wish gains strength, it can come to influence everything we think, say and do.

The question is not only whether we want to serve, but how we do so. There is a huge difference between the service that wears us down and even burns us out, and the service that uplifts, energises and gives us joy. What is the spark that is missing? What do we need to attend to?

There is satisfaction in carrying out an act of service with beauty and simplicity, and with no expectation of reward. Sometimes an offer of help feels more like a transaction, laden with unspoken conditions or expectations. There can be uneasiness and a knot in the stomach after what seemed to be a kind action. If we are not able to offer service in an open and loving way, is it better not to offer at all?

The surprising clue to loving service may lie in the second half of the 'golden rule' – to love and serve others as we love and serve ourselves. Is it possible to contribute to the well-being of others if we are neglecting our own well-being? To create an atmosphere of love and harmony if we have lost the taste of this ourselves? If service is an expression of love, then we must also love and serve ourselves. Our own happiness and that of others goes hand in hand.

**CHALLENGE:** Are you feeling burnt out, with nothing left to give? Do you offer service to others at the expense of your own well-being? Do something in the next week to show compassion to yourself. Try to bring the same softness and compassion into the next thing you do for someone else.

## REFLECTION

- Find a quiet space where you can relax. Sit comfortably. To help you settle, focus your awareness on your breathing. Let go of any thoughts, images or feelings that arise. Whenever you become distracted, bring your awareness gently back to the sensation of the breath going in and out. Spend a few minutes enjoying the experience of coming to rest.

- Call to mind all your close 'friends.' You can do this either by listing their names silently in your mind, or visualising them one by one; whatever method works best for you.

- Is it possible that our 'friends' are simply the people who do what we want? Ask yourself why you consider these people to be 'friends.' Explore the possibility that 'friends' are the people who behave in the way that is most comfortable for you. If you experience some resistance to this idea gently acknowledge and identify it. Test the idea out by reflecting on a relationship that has changed recently – what happened?

- Next, call to mind the people who are your adversaries – the people who make you feel a bit itchy when you think of them. What is it about them that makes them so challenging? Is it because they don't do what you want? Again, you may notice some resistance to this idea: gently acknowledge it and identify it. 'I'm resisting this.' Stay very soft and feel where the resistance is in your mind and body.

- Now, scan all the 'neutral' people in your world – those who have not had a personal impact on you yet. Why are they neutral? Is it because you have not yet classified them? Pick one of these people and ask yourself, 'Would she do what I wanted if I asked her?' Notice what happens.

- Reflect on the way that you divide people into 'friend', 'adversary' or 'neutral person.' How well does this serve you? How does it affect the way that you relate to them and offer them service? What would happen if you related to everybody with an open heart instead? Run through the scenario in your mind. Imagine yourself relating to people daily with a totally open heart, unconditionally, without expectations, without judgement. What would this be like?

- If you arrive at any conclusions, sit with them and let them deepen.

- Close with the wish 'May all beings be happy!'

## RESOURCES

www.thekingcentre.org was set up by Mrs Coretta Scott King as the living memorial and institutional guardian of Dr. Martin Luther King Jr.'s legacy.

The Autobiography of Martin Luther King Jr, edited by Clayborne Carson, is compiled from Martin Luther King's own words (London: Abacus, 2000).

Martin Luther King Jr, The Words of Martin Luther King, Jr, edited by Coretta Scott King (New York, NY: Newmarket Press, 2001).

You can listen to Martin Luther King Jr's 'I Have a Dream' speech on www.youtube.com or via www.mlkonline.net.

'Dr. Martin Luther King – A Historical Perspective', (released as a DVD in 2005 by Delta Home Entertainment) is one of several documentaries about Martin Luther King Jr.

'IF YOU UNDERSTAND AND YOU ARE DISTURBED, THEN YOU ARE MOVED TO ACTION.
THAT'S EXACTLY WHAT HAPPENED TO ME'
WANGARI MAATHAI, KENYA

# 16 COURAGE

## WHAT IS COURAGE?

Courage is about stretch. It's about seeing, feeling or realizing that something more or different can be done, developing the determination to do it, and then carrying it through despite all obstacles. We know in our bodies when we've been courageous. There is a glow of satisfaction and relief. Something has shifted, and we have grown in size.

Courage is not defined by what we do, but what we overcome within ourselves. It comes in many forms. It is found in a steady approach to everyday difficulties as well as in the single spontaneous gesture. It is happening quietly all around us as well as in the news.

Courage involves acknowledging our fears, but not being deterred from offering something that goes beyond our own immediate needs and comfort. Most courageous people have decided that the well-being of others is more important than their own, and have allowed this decision to drive their actions and the way they live. Invariably, they seem to find their own happiness in the process.

## WHY WANGARI MAATHAI?

As a child, Wangari Maathai was always a strong personality. She grew up in a traditional Kikuyu homestead in the Kenyan highlands, and tells of her many adventures working in the fields, collecting firewood and going to market. She started off walking barefoot to school yet became the first woman in East and Central Africa to receive a doctorate. She was persecuted during the regime of Daniel Arap Moi but subsequently became a member of the Kenyan government. The Greenbelt Movement which she started in the 1970s has now planted over thirty million trees across Kenya, and takes as its goal the entire re-greening of Africa.

Concern and compassion is the driving force of Professor Maathai's life. Having experienced the suffering of her family and community, when they lost their livelihood and their land became deforested, she has devoted her life to addressing these problems on a wider scale. Her initial concern with the environment then led her to become active in areas such as women's rights, tribal reconciliation and democratic reform. One thing led to another. 'Throughout my life I have never stopped to strategize about my next steps. I often just keep walking along, through whichever door opens. I have been on a journey and this journey never stops.'

Wangari Maathai's life has not lacked heartbreak and adversity. Her husband divorced her, saying she was too strong-minded. She has been frequently attacked in the newspapers and imprisoned. She has often been in physical danger. 'What people see as fearlessness is really persistence. Because I am focused on the situation, I don't see danger. Because I don't see danger, I don't allow my mind to imagine what might happen to me, which is my definition of fear.' Instead, she emphasises the need to be patient and determined. 'None of us can control every situation we find ourselves in. What we can control is how we react when things turn against us. I have always seen failure as a challenge to pull myself up and keep going.'

**'COURAGE IS BEING SCARED TO DEATH, BUT SADDLING UP ANYWAY' JOHN WAYNE, USA**

Wangari Maathai stresses that her achievements, and her Nobel Peace Prize, are not hers alone. Typically, she does this through an analogy with nature: 'A great river always begins somewhere...but for the stream to grow into a river, it must meet other tributaries and join them as it heads for a lake or a sea.' Her courage seems to be rooted in this capacity to be grounded and humble. 'No matter how powerful we become in government or how many awards we receive, our power and strength and our ability to reach our goals depend on the people, those whose work remains unseen, who are the soil out of which we grow, the shoulders on which we stand.'

## HOW DOES COURAGE LEAD TO HAPPINESS?

Courage fuels our motivation to act on what we care about. We tap into energy that we didn't know was there and we may be surprised by the difference our words and actions can make. It reminds us that life is something precious and exciting. It is often when we are challenged that we feel most happy and alive.

**'WE MUST BE WILLING TO LET GO OF THE LIFE WE HAVE PLANNED, SO AS TO ACCEPT THE LIFE THAT IS WAITING FOR US' JOSEPH CAMPBELL, USA**

Courage can be compelling, exhilarating and contagious. It acknowledges that life is full of difficulties, but also shows they can be overcome. If someone else has demonstrated this already, moving ahead despite their fear, then perhaps we can follow. It boosts our confidence in what human beings are capable of.

**TRUE STORY:** Vedran Smailovic was one of the hundreds of thousands of Bosnians who lived through the bombings, sniper fire and shortages of the siege of Sarajevo. In 1992, after 22 people had been killed while queuing for bread, he decided to offer 'a musical prayer for peace.' Ignoring the gunfire that threatened his life, he played his cello for 22 days in the bomb crater where they had died. Smailovic also became famous for playing for free at funerals, even though these were often targeted by Serb forces. His 'Music for Peace' initiative became an inspiration for civil resistance in Bosnia, and the place where he first played has become a roadside shrine to the power of the human spirit.

We all know what it feels like when courage is absent, when we keep silent or avoid a task that calls out to us. Our shoulders slump a little and our head drops down. Whereas if we can overcome our anxiety and resistance, it brings an inner victory.

Not many of us will play a prominent role in national or global affairs. But each person can display courage in standing up for what they believe in, however difficult or unpopular. If each of us is born with a unique voice and part to play then what happens if we choose not to make use of them? Sometimes we need to do more, not less, to think big, not small. Every avalanche starts with a single snowflake.

The people who are featured in this book are human, not superhuman. Many were born with no particular advantages or skills. What they all have in common was that they found the courage to ask themselves what they wanted, or what they could not accept, and then searched for the next step with all the wisdom they possessed. What they all decided was that it was impossible to lead a happy life without working for the happiness of others.

It can feel scary to say 'I want to be happy!' We may have been taught that this is selfish and inappropriate. Yet it is difficult for unhappy people to inspire others, to get things moving, or to bring about change.

**'GENIUS? NOTHING! STICKING TO IT IS THE GENIUS! I'VE FAILED MY WAY TO SUCCESS'**
THOMAS EDISON, USA

Seeking our own happiness, using all the intelligence we possess, is invariably the most honest and effective starting point for a meaningful life.

To make the most of life, it is helpful to reflect on death. Life is so compelling that even thinking about death is an act of courage in itself. Yet nothing is more certain than the fact that we will die, and nothing is less certain than the moment of our death. Facing up to this unarguable truth can help to overcome the fears that hold us back.

It can also be productive to stand back and assess our fears and anxieties. Some are a warning bell, to keep us safe from danger. But others are no more than an emotion, born of culture and habit. Confront a fear, and its power fades a little. It may be showing us where our edge is, and where we can grow. Can we develop the skill of approaching our fears with sensitivity but without needing to run away?

**'COURAGE IS THE PRICE THAT LIFE EXACTS FOR GRANTING PEACE' AMELIA EARHART, USA**

It takes courage not just to get motivated and underway, but also to do our best from start to finish, and rejoice in that. It also takes courage to accept that we may not be able to live up to the standards that we set ourselves. Every action carries its own risks and rewards.

Sometimes the greatest courage demanded from us is simply to keep going with a task that we find difficult or discouraging. Where does the strength come from to do this? Is that strength always there, if we dig deep enough? Can we genuinely learn from mistakes and difficulties – not just say or pretend that we do? This also takes courage.

Everyone has something to give, in tiny moments, in simple gestures. There are endless opportunities. Who is to say what is most important, or where each action will lead? Simply to make one person's life better or easier is a step towards making the world a better place for everyone. And in courageously stretching to help others be happy, we are likely to find happiness for ourselves.

May you be happy. May all beings be happy.

**CHALLENGE:** Is there something worthwhile that you long to accomplish? What is it that holds you back? How substantial is that fear? Even if you're afraid, are you willing to do it anyway? Commit to something now.

## REFLECTION

- Find a quiet space where you can relax. Sit comfortably. To help you settle, focus your awareness on your breathing. Let go of any thoughts, images or feelings that arise. Whenever you become distracted, bring your awareness gently back to the sensation of the breath going in and out. Spend a few minutes enjoying the experience of coming to rest.

● Begin with a scan of your body. Start with the feet, which keep you balanced and allow you to stand upright on the ground. Move up through the calves and thighs, which give you the power to walk and perhaps to run. Let your attention pass over the belly and intestines, which process and digest the food that fuels you. Move upwards across your breasts and shoulders. Down your arms to your hands, with their capacity to give and take. Feel the strength of your neck and spinal column, which hold you erect.

● Pass your attention across your face, with its endless capacity to smile and laugh, or to wince and cry. Notice the expressiveness of the muscles in your cheek and the flexibility of your mouth. Reflect on the technical sophistication of your eyes and ears. Even if your body is not as functional as you would like, it is still miraculous and extraordinary.

● Bring your attention back to the breath that passes lightly through your lips and nostrils. Watch how it comes and it goes, without any effort or interference on your part. What will happen when this fragile breath stops? However scary it feels, can you face the reality that one day your life will end?

● Now reflect on all the people and animals who have already died today. Consider how they woke up this morning, just as you did, but are now dead. Perhaps their death was completely unexpected, due to a heart attack, a car accident or a sudden sickness. Perhaps it was simply due to old age. They had plans for today, and plans for the future, just as you do, but now everything is over for them.

● How does it feel to be alive? What do you want to do with the opportunities that this brings? What is it that matters most to you? Can you find the courage to get on with it?

● Close with the wish 'May all beings be happy!'

## RESOURCES

www.greenbeltmovement.org is the official website of the Green Belt Movement and of Professor Wangari Maathai.

Wangari Maathai, Unbowed: One Woman's Story (London: Heinemann, 2007).

Wangari Maathai, The Green Belt Movement: Sharing the Approach and the Experience (New York: Lantern Books, 2006).

There are various short videos of Wangari Maathai on www.youtube.com.

# Notes

Every effort has been made to trace the copyright holders of material quoted in this book. We would like to thank the many people worldwide who assisted in this process. If application is made in writing to the publisher, any omissions will be included in future editions.

## 01 HUMILITY (HELEN KELLER)

Image quotation courtesy of the American Foundation for the Blind, Helen Keller Archives. Used with permission. Other quotations are from: Helen Keller, *To Love This Life: Quotations*, (2000), copyright American Foundation for the Blind. All rights reserved.

## 02 PATIENCE (HIS HOLINESS THE DALAI LAMA)

Quotations are from: The 14th Dalai Lama, *Ancient Wisdom Modern World: Ethics for a New Millennium* (London: Little, Brown, 1999). Permission granted by the publisher.

## 03 CONTENTMENT (MAHATMA GANDHI)

Permission to reproduce quotations granted by the Navajivan Trust, Ahmedabad, Gujarat, India.

## 04 DELIGHT (JANE GOODALL)

Quotations are from *www.janegoodall.org.*

## 05 KINDNESS (MOTHER TERESA)

Permission to reproduce quotations granted by the Missionaries of Charity, London, UK.

## 06 HONESTY (MUHAMMAD YUNUS)

Quotations are from Muhammed Yunus, *Banker to the Poor* (Cambridge, MA: Public Affairs Books, 2003). Permission to reproduce quotations granted by the publisher.

## 07 GENEROSITY (CÉSAR CHÁVEZ)

Permission to reproduce quotations granted by the César E. Chávez Foundation, *www.chavezfoundation.org*.

## 08 RIGHT SPEECH (CHIEF JOSEPH)

Permission to use the image and words of Chief Joseph granted by the Nez Perce Tribal Government: 'With much grateful appreciation that our grandfather's teachings continue' (from the descendants of Chief Joseph).

## 09 RESPECT (ALBERT EINSTEIN)

Permission to reproduce quotations granted by the Einstein Archive, Hebrew University of Jerusalem, Israel. Quotations are from: Albert Einstein, *What I Believe* (1930); reprinted in: *Ideas and Opinions* (The World As I See It). (Condor Books, 2005) and Walter Isaacson, *Einstein: His Life and Universe* (London: Simon & Schuster, 2007).

## 10 FORGIVENESS (DESMOND TUTU)

Quotations are from: John Allen, *Rabble Rouser for Peace* (New York: Free Press, 2006); permission granted by the publisher. Image quotation reproduced with permission from The Forgiveness Project, *www.forgivenessproject.com*.

## 11 GRATITUDE (RAM DASS)

With thanks to The Ram Dass Foundation, *www.ramdass.org*.

## 12 LOYALTY (AUNG SAN SUU KYI)

Quotations are from: Aung San Suu Kyi, *Freedom from Fear*, edited by Michael Aris (London:Viking, 1991); permission granted by Penguin Books Ltd.

## 13 ASPIRATION (CRAIG KIELBURGER)

Quotations are reproduced with permission from Free the Children, *www.freethechildren.com*.

## 14 PRINCIPLES (ALBERT SCHWEITZER)

Quotations are from: Albert Schweitzer, *Memoirs of Childhood and Youth*, translated by Kurt Bergel and Alice R. Bergel, (Syracuse, NY: Syracuse University Press, 1997) and from: Albert Schweitzer, *Reverence for Life*, (London: SPCK Press, 1966).

## 15 SERVICE (MARTIN LUTHER KING JR.)

Quotations are from: *The Words of Martin Luther King, Jr.*, selected by Coretta Scott King (New York: Newmarket Press, 1987).

## 16 COURAGE (WANGARI MAATHAI)

Quotations are from: Wangari Maathai, *Unbowed: One Woman's Story* (London: William Heinemann, 2007); reproduced with permission from the Random House Group Ltd.